The Greatest Fall of All

by Ed Tonore

Prologue

As I stood to leave the stadium with two minutes left I looked up in the nighttime sky and something magical happened. Looking towards the lights I saw what I had waited sixty-one years to see. Snowflakes! I had always dreamed of seeing a college football game in the snow. Okay, so it was inside the two-minute mark, and I was leaving my seat, but still I took it as an omen.

Something good was in the air for this 2017 college football season. I don't know that most people feel the same way I do about watching snow fall during a game, but being

from the Deep South, it's a dream I'd had my whole life. As I

left the venerable old stadium I could hear the band and

remaining fans singing that song again. The most famous fight

song of all.

Cheer Cheer for old Notre Dame,

Wake up the echoes cheering her name...

I am a longtime LSU fan, but growing up in a Catholic

family with many Catholic aunts, uncles and cousins we also

always pulled for Notre Dame. I've always been an LSU fan,

but I'm even more of a *college* football fan and this is my

story, the story of a college football season, and how this fan

enjoyed it.

Sports is one of the most influential dynamics of our

lives. We play it, we watch it, we experience emotional ups and

downs because of it. Whether you're nervously watching a

loved one play, reminiscing about when you were on the field yourself, or just following your favorite team, sports is

undeniably woven into the fabric of our existence.

Man has invented many sports to play and watch, but

for me crowds, the color, the pageantry and traditions of

American college football cannot be matched. One fan fact is

that most people are knowledgeable about their favorite

university's football traditions, but have only a passing

understanding of the wonderful traditions at other college

football programs from all over the country. Until you sit in

Brigham Young stadium with the Wasatch mountains as a

backdrop, tailgated on a boat in the Tennessee river before a

Tennessee matchup, or watched and listened to the horn section

of the Notre Dame band play under the Gold Dome, you can't

fully appreciate what game day wonders are happening all over

our great nation. The passion and intensity that college football

fans pour into the allegiance to their teams is only matched by

international soccer.

But, answer me this: Do soccer matches have a live tiger in a cage rolling around the field before they start? Or a live buffalo charging onto the field? Do soccer teams have huge precision marching bands to stir the imagination pregame and perform intricate formations at intermission? Do soccer teams have beautiful cheerleaders? Do they have midnight yell practice with 80,000 screaming fans? Do soccer matches have tailgates lowered and tents raised with carefully prepared cuisine fit for a king? I know the answer. It's NO!

And don't get me started on how exciting a 1-0 soccer game can be. About as dull as a dollar pocket knife. By the numbers, international soccer may be the world's most popular sport, but American college football is the world's greatest game on any field of play. Wait, someone said just asked, "What about PRO Football?"

Never head of it. Didn't know it existed.

If I had to guess, we're probably talking about a bunch

of spoiled rich athletes who won't stand for our national

anthem, nor even know the words to it. Probably all about

"show me the money" and team loyalty is synonymous with

"long gone."

Okay, so I do know pro football. And, sure, not all the

players are like that, but, lately those who are have been their

own worst enemy. Nope, college football is the "bomb" and

this means "really good" in today's jargon.

I originally discovered my love for college football

when I was seven years old. My mother and stepfather took me

to a Louisiana State University (LSU) game in 1957. My

stepfather got tickets to the LSU/Mississippi State game late in

the year when his boss at Yawn Manufacturing Company, a

steel fabrication company in Baton Rouge, gave them to him.

Seems the boss's nephew was playing for LSU and he had

player's tickets. When I asked who the player was so I could

follow him, my stepfather said some sophomore by the name

of Billy Cannon. Since freshmen couldn't play back then, this was Cannon's first varsity season and he had been doing very well. Mississippi State won 14-6 but that didn't dampen my spirits. To me the crowd, the band and a tiger in his cage on the sideline were more exciting than the Zephyr roller coaster ride at Pontchartrain Beach in New Orleans.

Cannon went on to win the Heisman Trophy award in 1959. He became my hero after we were invited to his house and he threw the football to me and we took pictures. The Heisman Trophy is given each year to the most outstanding college player. That's taking the top spot from some 20,000 plus college football players. Cannon was still my hero even after he got busted and served time for counterfeiting money. After all, he said people got him into bad investments and he needed money for his family.

Forty years later at an LSU booster club meeting in Jackson, Mississippi, where Cannon was the guest speaker I thanked him for that day. With a lump in my throat, I stood up and described how kind and generous he and his wife had been

to me when I was nine years old. The assembled crowd oohed

and ahhhed, and said, *How nice.* But Cannon's response to my

story was not well received. "Man," he said, "I must be getting

real old when some old gray-haired dude says he was a kid

when I won the Heisman."

"Hero no more, Counterfeit Cannon!" was what I

thought. But I kept it to myself, so he could have his comic

moment before the crowd.

After the LSU Tigers only broke even in 1957, winning

five games and losing five, not much was expected from the

team in 1958. But when my Tigers began winning game after

game, the whole hometown of Baton Rouge, where I lived, and

the rest of Louisiana began hyperventilating over prospects for

a shot at the national title. It would be the first time in fifty

years. The excitement was contagious and my father came

down with a good case of Tiger Flu. Now he wanted to go to

every game, and he began taking me on the weekends. He

usually brought a cousin my age, and we would meet my uncle

Louis Tonore and his wife, Aunt Virginia. Uncle Louis was my

godfather, and I always felt like he was my second father.

I might nowadays forget things I did yesterday, but I'll

never forget those ballgames and everything I did with my dad

on those weekends. My father lived five hours away, but I was

seeing him almost weekly. Funny, how I still remember the

smallest detail about every visit these sixty years later. Our

favorite pregame place was The Pastime Lounge where we

would devour the best pizzas and po-boys in Baton Rouge. The

adults drank bourbon over ice or with water and we youngsters

sat in and soaked up their stories about what was happening

around the country in college football. Maybe I'd hear some

radio announcer over the speakers in the restaurant say

something like, "SMU beat UCLA today," and I'd say "Wow

cool!" It didn't matter that I had no clue what those letters

stood for. To me, the announcement sounded cooler than a

coke float.

My father never had tickets in advance. He always

waited and bought them from individuals standing around

outside the stadium. He would hold up two fingers, which

meant he was looking to buy two tickets. And he would only

buy them below face value. Just when I'd think we were ready

to go in and get our seats, he'd hold up the tickets, raise the

price, and resell them for a profit. The process was nerve

wracking to me. I was afraid we'd never get in. But, he'd work

his magic, and we'd have great tickets *and* he made enough

money to pay for our concessions and his gas for the ride

home. He also took the time to teach me how to patiently find

tickets, figure out the value based on availability, and how to

negotiate the price down. This childhood exercise in gridiron

capitalism would serve me well later in life.

It was during our wonderful time together at football

games that I began to hear my father talk about how before I

was born and shortly thereafter, he and some other guys would

sometimes pick out the best college football game in the South that was in driving distance and they'd go to that game. They

went without tickets but always got in and also made sure they

checked out the best eating spots in that town.

When I was in middle school, I began selling programs

at LSU games and my dad didn't come to as many games.

When I graduated from law school and opened a practice in

downtown Jackson, Mississippi, across from Hal & Mal's

restaurant, I could afford to buy season tickets to the LSU

games. But I couldn't get Big Ed to go anymore. Despite my

best efforts, no matter how I tempted him, he said his couch

was more comfortable. Plus, he could watch more games.

Also, he had remarried and had another son twelve

years younger than me. He was growing up in Dad's house. He

had responsibilities to my younger brother, Ronnie, and the

pull to meet me for a game had diminished. The years of our

game day weekends quietly melted away. But those wonderful

times when Big Ed and I did have together at the football

games were indelibly etched in my mind. And, when Dad got

older, I was able to talk him into going to a couple games.

Then, as I, too, have grown older, I see how we're able to have

a clearer understanding of life and what's really important. I

think Big Ed realized how important it had been to me, and to

him, too.

The last game he attended with me was the LSU/

Alabama game in 1996. He had become very weak. A friend of

mine who was a member of the LSU support group Tiger

Athletic Foundation got us tickets in the lower seats and close

walking distance from our tailgate. I could tell his knees and

back were hurting bad, and I wasn't sure if he'd make it.

Maybe he soldiered-up knowing how much it meant to me, and

that it could be our last game day stand. To add to Big Ed's

pain Alabama won 26-0. I was afraid he'd never make the walk

back. But as we left the stadium a few minutes before the end,

I hailed a car, hoping to catch a ride. When the car stopped and

the window rolled down, I was astonished to see the driver was

none other than John Ferguson. He was the longtime "Voice of the Tigers" who was now retired. John broadcasted LSU sports for over forty years and during his tenure I had occasion to pick him up more than once at the Jackson airport for booster club meetings. He looked at me from behind the wheel and said, "Ed from Jackson. How are you doing? Need some help?"

John drove us back to the tailgate where we "went to the whip." That's a horse racing term taught to me by my good friend Pete Daschbach. It means you need a strong drink to help you to the finish line, and I don't mean ginger ale with a cherry. Ten months later Dad passed away, just two days after his only grandchild, my son Eddie, was born. He'd hung on doggedly and fought his medical problems for six months longer than the doctor thought he could. The doctor said, "I think he just wanted to hear he had a grandchild." When told he had a grandson and he was named after him, Dad cried. "Tell that boy to always call me Pap Paw," he said. Then he took his rest and gave in and left me with good memories of

our times together.

Two months after my father was buried I went to

Tuscaloosa for the LSU/Alabama game hoping for revenge.

When the final horn sounded, I could imagine Big Ed smiling

down. The Tigers won by one more point than Bama had beat

us the previous year while Dad had watched. My friends and I

lingered in the upper deck long after the game. We couldn't

take our eyes off the scoreboard: 27-0. Somebody said, "Lets

have a toast to Big Ed." So we took a shot of Wild Turkey

bourbon, Dad's favorite, and then poured some on the seats in

front of us for the old man's shot.

In the days and weeks after that game, my mind would

drift sometimes back to those glory days, and I'd recall our

conversations about him making those road trips to the biggest

game in the south once or twice a year. And the idea took hold

and grew in my mind, that it would be an exciting, and once-

in-a-lifetime experience if I could honor Dad by taking his idea to another level and go to the biggest game in the whole country. And the idea snowballed. I would go to the biggest game EVERY weekend, from the season opener all the way though to the national championship.

Of course, I was all keyed up, and I couldn't wait to share this idea with all my friends and family. My wife's response was a long stare. Silent, like she was waiting for some punchline. I said, "I'm not joking."

She said, "Ok, but I'm not sure I can make that many games."

My cousin Todd's response was, "You're too old for that. You'll wear out before November."

My friend Glenn Roper's response was, "Are you crazy? Do you know how expensive and difficult that will be?" He paused, grinned, and said, "But if you do it put me down for the Army/Navy game."

My son Eddie's response was predictable. "Cool! I'm

going."

Sometimes you just have to have a leap of faith that

things will work out. "And when it happens," I said, "I'll call it

The Greatest Fall of All."

My daughter Savannah said, "You need to write a blog

each week so people can read along and enjoy your

experiences." What the hell is a blog? I asked her. I told her it

sounds like how I feel after eating my weight during the

holidays. But, turns out, a blog is where you write heartfelt

things and you hope your kids don't post them on Insta-

Dummy. And after getting a lesson on blogging, so I could

actually do it myself, I was ready to blog my fingers off. All I

had to do next was get started.

It helped that my wife Jenny is a BIG college football

fan to start with. Her dad Ollie Keller (Poppa) played on the

1951 National Championship team for Tennessee and coached

at various major colleges. He was head coach at University of

Louisiana Monroe, called Northeast Louisiana University back

then. Poppa instilled in his children, Katie, Kevin, Lucy and

my wife Jenny, a competitive desire to succeed, and all of them

did. Poppa wanted to go on this odyssey with us, but was

eighty-eight and too weak to travel very far or for very long.

So I hoped I could honor him as well as Big Ed with this idea.

Poppa had also served on one of the most illustrious

coaching staffs in college football history when he was at Iowa

State. It included Jimmy Johnson who went on to win a

national championship as the head coach at Miami, and two

Super Bowls as the head coach with the Dallas Cowboys.

Johnny Majors was at Iowa State with Poppa and won a

national championship at Pittsburgh and was head coach at the

University of Tennessee for fifteen years. Jackie Sherrill was

there, too, and he became head coach at Pittsburgh, and later at

Mississippi State. Jackie became the first "million dollar"

coach when Texas A&M hired him away from Pittsburgh. Joe

Alvazano was there, too, at Iowa State and became one of the

longest tenured coaches in the NFL.

There's more football in the family. Our son-in-law

Robert Lane played quarterback (QB) and tight end at Ole

Miss, which is the University of Mississippi. And, like family

to me, is my library dedicated to college football. It's further

evidence of the passion around our house. I make claim that

it's the largest private college football library. I will continue to

say it until proven otherwise. And if you think you know a

contender for my library, you'd better have more than a

thousand books about this sport.

The year of the 2017 season would mark sixty-one

years in a row I attended LSU games. Now, when that year

would be over I would also hope to win the National

Championship of College Football blogging. Maybe I'd get a

trophy. It was time to get this party started cause Big Ed had

been waiting for me to "wake up the echoes" since 1997. And

on the twentieth anniversary of his death, Big Ed would ride with me around the country, the very spirit of the game that he

enjoyed so much, the sport he introduced me to and that I love

still. Along with about forty million others who love college

football, this book is for everyone of you.

GLOSSARY OF FOOTBALL TERMS

If even three of my readers are not your run-of-the-mill and

foaming-at-the-mouth football fanatics, I think a short

explanation of relevant football terms will be helpful.

COLLEGE FOOTBALL NATIONAL CHAMPIONSHIP

The last game of the season where the winner becomes the *Big*

Kahuna, *Big Cheese*, *Kingfish*, or whatever name you want to

apply to the Top Dog.

COLLEGE FOOTBALL PLAYOFF (CFP)

The top four teams in the final CFP poll is named by the CFP

Committee. These thirteen committee members are the czars of

our sport, and until we have a palace coup they will continue to

tell us who the final four teams are, and also how they are

matched up in two semi-final games. Those winners then play

for the championship.

BOWL GAMES

After the regular season ends, some schools are invited to a

cool party called a bowl game. It is usually held at some

desirable location where the players and coaches take in the

sights, have eating contests, stay up past curfew, and are

generally rewarded with gifts and a good time for a good

season. Sometimes the locations aren't as desirable, like

Shreveport, Birmingham, Memphis or El Paso. And sometimes

the team's season wasn't so good and are invited to play even

when they don't have a winning record. But if a city wants to

throw a cool party, there's no shortage of teams willing to show

up.

HEISMAN TROPHY

This trophy, named after John Heisman a famous player and

coach, is awarded every year to the player chosen the best

athlete out of the 20,000-plus players in college football. To

win this award you must have astounding statistics, be on a

winning team that's on TV a lot and hope the guys on ESPN

GameDay like you.

ESPN GameDay

Every Saturday in the fall a crew of experts has a television

show in the morning where they discuss that day's games,

show human interest stories, and pick the winning teams for

that day (which are usually wrong except for the camera man

Bear's picks). The cast is actually very well-versed and the

human interest stories are good enough to win awards. They

usually choose what they feel is the most important game of

the week as a location for the show, and also usually have a

guest picker, someone to predict the winners of the day. I've

been checking my mailbox and emails but haven't yet been

invited to showcase my own prognosticating skills. Not sure

what the holdup is, 'cause I know I can pick football games

better than Katie Perry, Lance Armstrong or Mark Cuban, who were all previous pickers.

NATIONAL FOOTBALL LEAGUE (NFL)

This is the pro league where the best college players get to continue suiting up for the game they love, and get paid vast sums of money. They also usually get to tell the coaches what to do, and are faced with tough decisions like whether or not to stand for the national anthem. They must also figure out how not to get lost in their massive homes. Before you ask for an autograph, be sure to ask "how much?" Because you might not be able to afford it. By the way, some NFL players, however, are very involved in their communities and are all-around cool dudes.

OFFENSE

When one team controls the football and tries to move it downfield to score, they are on offense. The spectacle is kinda like watching Brad Pitt work his way through a crowded club.

DEFENSE

The team on defense tries aggressively to stop the other team's offense from scoring, and to get the ball back for themselves. Kinda like watching Brad Pitt bump into Angelina Jolie in that club.

QUARTERBACK (QB)

This is the player in charge of the offense. He is usually the one the head cheerleader and the gold-digging sorority girl chase for different reasons. One wants Love and one wants a Lamborghini.

LAND GRANT COLLEGE

A land grant college or university is an institution of higher learning designated by a state to receive the benefits of the Morill Acts of 1862 and 1890. These acts funded universities in many states by granting federal lands to states, which could

then sell the land to raise money to build colleges dedicated to

the pursuit of agriculture, science, engineering and military

science. Examples are the University of Georgia, Auburn

University, University of Tennessee, Louisiana State

University, Florida State University, Penn State University,

Michigan State University, and many others around the

country. Guess you could call this the first welfare program in

U.S. history, and one that worked well. A shame congress can

no longer seem to pass legislation as broadly beneficial to its

citizens as this.

ASSOCIATED PRESS POLL (AP POLL)

Since 1936, a panel of sportswriters and broadcasters have

voted each week during the football season on which are the

top 25 teams in the country. ESPN GameDay uses this poll to

help determine where they will broadcast from each week.

However, sometimes their trucks get lost and windup in places

like New York or Harrisonburg, Va. The panel of sixty-one

voters only sometimes watches the games, they rarely look at statistics, and seem partial to their favorite teams. The panel members are, however, exceptional at finding for themselves the maximum expenses their employers will allow for food and drink. For these reasons this poll has been accepted as the most respected football poll over the years. Now, with the CFP in place, the AP poll rules only until late October each year when the CFP committee begins its poll.

WEEK MINUS-ONE: THE PRESEASON KICKOFF PARTY

Every year on the Saturday before Labor Day weekend we throw a huge preseason football party at our house in Fairhope, Alabama, a charming town on the eastern shore of Mobile Bay named by *Southern Living Magazine* in its April, 2018, issue as the 2nd best small town in the South to live in behind Aiken, South Carolina. It's a great party , with great food, wonderful bands and as many as three hundred friends and relatives combine to make it the most anticipated house party of the year. Okay, so I'm biased, but that's also what everyone says

who shows up.

'Course there are lots of adult beverages flowing, but I

think the real fun is the anticipation of the beginning of

football season. Everyone wears their team's colors and last

year, in 2017, there were twenty-four different universities

represented. For the party, I printed a poster showing the games

I would be going to on my odyssey if the preseason rankings

held up all year. It was just an example because we knew that

wouldn't happen. There are always upsets and teams that

would play worse than anticipated and some teams would do

better than expected. So, as the rankings changed my itinerary

would change every week. Still, our guests could get an idea of

the scope of my travel plans.

All night at the party you heard "Geaux Tigers" and

"Roll Tide" and "War Eagle" and "Go Vols" and plenty of

other war cries ringing out through the massive Spanish moss-

covered live oaks on our street, and echoing all the way across the bay to let everyone know The Greatest Fall of All was

almost here!

Kicking off the "Greatest Fall of All" at the College Football Hall of Fame

WEEK ONE: ALABAMA VS FLORIDA STATE
MERCEDES-BENZ STADIUM
ATLANTA, GEORGIA
SEPTEMBER 2, 2017

The Hype

Red Elephants vs. Seminoles
Mentor vs. Pupil

Alabama under Bear Bryant and Nick Saban has ruled college

football. Alabama won four of the last eight national

championships under coach Saban and six during Bryant's 25-

year tenure from 1958 to 1982.

Florida State didn't experience success in football till

Bobby Bowden showed up in 1976. Before Bowden became

coach, Florida State football was so bad the players were called

CERs (Co-Ed Repellents). Under coach Bowden, a southern

gentleman if there ever was one, the Seminoles proceeded to

win two National Championships and finish in the top five

ranking for an unprecedented thirteen years in a row. A devout

Christian, coach Bowden is now a highly sought-after

motivational speaker.

Now under coach Jimbo Fisher, who became the head

coach in 2010, the Seminoles have won one national

championship and eighty-two percent of their games. Before

the game, this matchup was billed as the greatest season opener

in college football history. No.1 Alabama vs No. 3 Florida

State was the first time the season opened with a matchup

between teams ranked this high. Two weeks before the game,

tickets were selling on eBay from $700 to $3000.

My son Eddie and I got tickets on StubHub at a better

price once the game got closer. We became more excited once

our tickets were in hand, and then kept at a fever pitch with the

game being advertised constantly on ESPN. Finally, come

game day, downtown Atlanta was jammed with Florida State

and Alabama fans screaming their notorious "War Chant" and

"Roll Tide." Eddie and I couldn't think of a better way to kick

off The Greatest Fall of All.

The Hall of Fame

If you love college football, the College Football Hall of Fame

is a mecca. Inspiring, informative, and very interactive. It's a

must see for all ages whether you are a fan or not. The movie

we watched while visiting the museum had everyone yelling

and singing and getting fired up for the game. Whether it's the

collection of memorabilia, the presentation of the history and

traditions of each school, or the various interactive rooms,

you're sure to have a great time!

The Food

Saturday morning, Eddie and I chowed down at Goldberg's

Bagel and Deli.

Howard Aaron immigrated from South Africa in 1981 and bought Goldberg's. Since then, it has expanded to six stores in the greater Atlanta area, and is opening in New Orleans and other major southern cities next year. Goldberg's has become an Atlanta tradition for the last thirty-five years and I would recommend it to anyone. As a parting gift, Howard gave us a bag of biltong, South African beef jerky that tastes a lot like ours, but a little more peppery.

Our lunch spot was the most popular pizza place in Atlanta, Antico. The pizzas and pasta are so Italian that the prices are listed in Euros and Dollars.

After the game, we hit The Varsity for Chili Slawdawgs and Frosty Oranges. Unless you have been in a cave for a long time, you know The Varsity is an iconic Atlanta stop, and has been around for the last eighty-six years. It's across from Georgia Tech and is the largest drive-in fast food restaurant in the world.

There is no shortage of fine dining in Atlanta, but Eddie

and I had to get back to college and work, so we decided to

wait till the National Championship or SEC conference

championship to spend more time exploring Atlanta's hotspots,

And I'm not talking about Cheetah or the Gold Club. If you

don't know what they are, that's a good thing.

The Game

Poppa, my father in law, said he learned during his coaching

career that to have a great defense "you have to be strong up

the middle." The defensive tackles, middle linebacker and

safeties must be dominant. And like all Nick Saban teams, this

one would prove it *was* ready for prime time.

As we entered the new Mercedes-Benz stadium, we

were amazed at the architecture, the giant circular video

screen, and the overall beauty and lighting that was built into

the design. I have been to Cowboy Stadium, otherwise known

as Jerry's World, and would say that this stadium is just as

good or better.

Now let's play some football. The first half of the

biggest opener in history lived up to its billing. In the second

half, however, Florida State imploded with a block punt,

fumbled kick-off return, and an interception all a the matter of

two minutes. The fat lady started singing. No sense in beating a

dead horse, or a Seminole, but Alabama tackled, ran, blocked

and kicked better. Their "Jimmy's and Joe's" could beat Jimbo

Fisher's X's and O's ten out of ten times this year.   **FINAL**

SCORE: ALABAMA 24, FLORIDA STATE 7

The Fans

College football fans tend to generalize about fans from the

other teams. Bama fans are "Rednecks", Tennessee and

Arkansas fans are "Hillbillies", LSU fans are "Coonasses", and

Ole Miss fans are "Arrogant Elitist".

Truth is, when you take the time to stop and talk to fans

from the other team, you find that we are all more alike than

you think. A Florida State fan I met from Knoxville, by the

name of Dean, said that his grandfather played with my father-

in-law on the 1951 Tennessee Vols National Championship

team. He shared this blog adventure of mine with all of his

friends and invited us to visit in Knoxville.

Mary and John from Pensacola are Bama fans who

actually used to live in my hometown of Fairhope. They

insisted that we get together for dinner sometime.

Jan and her sorority sisters from Florida State said,

"There is no way someone can go to ALL of these games that

you say are going to. But if Florida State is again one of the

games, can we go?!" (Side note: My son "Little Eddie" said

that after years of careful study he is certain that Florida State

has the prettiest girls.)

Tailgating was sparse since the game was played in

downtown Atlanta, but there were a handful of impromptu

tailgates. I'm looking forward to next week when I can graze

from tailgate-to-tailgate at Ohio State.

WINNERS AND LOSERS

Winners

1) Alabama. An obvious choice. This team's on cruise control

until someone can stop the carnage

2) Howard. Howard made history by beating UNLV, even

though they were 45-point under dogs. Biggest upset in college

football history. **HOWARD 43, UNLV 40**

3) Liberty. Don't even know where it's at, but, they beat

Baylor. I hear they gave all the students "liberty" till mid-

terms. **LIBERTY 48, BAYLOR 45**

Losers

1) Florida. Their offense is worse than The French Army,

whose tanks only have two gears– both in reverse.

MICHIGAN 33, FLORIDA 17

2) Texas. Welcome to UT football Tom Herman (their new

coach). The dysfunctional culture in Austin may prove to take longer to change than the young genius thought. On a personal

note, I am still a fan. **MARYLAND 51, TEXAS 41**

3) BYU. Really? Minus 5 yards rushing? 96 total yards? LSU

had players with displaced families due to hurricane Harvey,

and fifteen scholarship players didn't dress out due to injuries

and suspensions, yet still they won. The game was much worse

than the score indicated.

LSU 27, BYU O

NEXT WEEK'S GAME: OKLAHOMA @ OHIO STATE

Ohio State should stay No. 2 and Oklahoma should move up to

No. 6. Looking forward to seeing a game in "The

Shoe" (Horseshoe), a.k.a Ohio State's stadium, and watching

their band in pregame performance dot the "i" in Ohio, spelled

out on the field.

Two great coaches, two storied programs, and two great

QB's looking to lead their teams to a NC, and maybe one of

them to win the Heisman trophy. Talk about mascot identity

crisis. Ohio State are the Buckeyes, and Oklahoma are the Sooners. What the heck is a buckeye or a sooner?

Is it game time yet?

NOTE: Please pray for the victims of Harvey and their continued recovery. Also pray for the victims and people in the path of Irma.

Pregame tradition: Dotting the "I"

**WEEK 2: OKLAHOMA VS. OHIO STATE
OHIO STADIUM
COLUMBUS, OHIO
SEPTEMBER 9, 2017**

The Hype

Sooners vs. Buckeyes
Seeking revenge vs. Seeking redemption

As the sun rose on the sprawling Ohio State campus, we were

met with beautiful skies and temperatures in the 50s. The town

was electric with anticipation of a rematch of last year's Ohio

State Buckeyes beat-down of the Oklahoma Sooners in

Norman, Oklahoma. Although fans of both teams were cordial

to each other Thursday and Friday nights in the nearby campus

pubs, there was detectable intensity in their eyes, laser-focused

like a big cat stalking its prey.

No. 2 Ohio State vs. No. 5 Oklahoma was the marquee

game of a weekend of big matchups. The winner would

catapult itself into becoming the main contender to dethrone

Clemson or beat No. 1 Alabama. In the 127-year history of

Buckeye football, they have never beaten a top five, non-

conference opponent at home.

Tickets were $200-$1,300, and were readily available

on StubHub and at the stadium. I've come to believe you can

get tickets regardless of how big the game is. These two teams

are two of the most storied programs in college football

history. The Buckeyes have won eight National Championships

and have had seven Heisman winners. Oklahoma has won

seven National Championships and has had five Heisman

winners. Last year Ohio State put a beat-down on the Sooners

in Norman, Oklahoma 45-24.

Big Ed said one of the most exciting games he ever went to was the 1950 Texas/Oklahoma game, known as the "Red River Shootout" because of the Red River running though both states. The annual game is always played at the Cotton Bowl stadium during the Texas State Fair. At that 1950 game on October 4th, Oklahoma won 14-13 in a real western shootout, and went on to win the NC. By my calculations, I was only four days old. Guess dad called an audible, and went to the game knowing I was in good hands and mom wouldn't fumble the little "football."

The Food

After Week One's blog, I got more questions about the food than about the game or the teams. Not sure what that says about our followers, but, here goes with the eats again.

Thursday, we ate at Eddie George's Grill. Eddie wasn't there, must not have heard we were coming. We had Heisman cocktails, fried deviled eggs, Supreme Mac & Cheese, and the best wings ever. Eddie was the Buckeyes 1995 Heisman

winner and one of the most beloved players ever. He is also a

successful entrepreneur and sports commentator.

Friday lunch was at The Blue Danube. A campus

favorite since 1940, blue plate specials and German food

highlight a diverse menu. Supper on Friday night was pub food

at The Varsity, the closest pub to the stadium. This is the most

popular and well-known hangout on game day weekends in

Columbus. Pizza was great and the beer ice cold. OU fans sung

"Boomer Sooner" and Buckeye fans sang their version of

"Hang On Sloopy". Also I'd recommend Buckeye Donuts on

the OSU campus. Great breakfast or late night place. Open all

night, they are known for their fresh-hot and creative versions

of doughnuts, and regular breakfast fare. Not sure why college

kid would want donuts between 1 and 5 am. Late night

studying?

The Fans

Thursday night we met Jonathon and his posse from Oklahoma. They were blown away that anyone would attempt an odyssey like ours. But, like almost everyone else we met, they immediately asked to follow the blog. Jonathon asked me where our next game would be and I said probably Louisville vs. Clemson. A big smile spread across his face, and he said, "My brother is a defensive coach for Clemson, and I can get you tickets." That made it easy. Don't think I wouldn't cash in on that deal.

Saturday we decided to go tailgate-to-tailgate and get down with our peoples. Almost everyone we met wanted the blog address, and I got tired of typing it in their phone. So we got a quick-print place to make business cards. Who knows, maybe this would turn into a *real* enterprise and we could get free peanuts or something.

Walking across from campus on Friday, we heard a loud commotion coming from a bar called The Thirst Scholar.

The place was packed with what looked like, of course, thirsty

scholars singing, "Hang on sloopy, sloppy hang on, O-H-I-O."

On Saturday, I wore my LSU visor and a buckeye

necklace. A buckeye, by the way, is a nut from the buckeye tree

that once dominated the Ohio State campus. Oklahoma is

called Sooners because of the Oklahoma Land Rush of 1889,

and Sooners were settlers who sneaked under cover of night to

get a head start on the official mad dash to claim some land.

Because of my LSU visor, many tailgaters asked, "Whats up

with you?" I was glad to explain. And usually got more

followers to my blog.

I was very impressed with the hospitality shown by the

many different tailgates we visited. The "Traveling Idiots"

were Rob, Denny and the Two Todds, all OSU grads who

loved to travel to away games. Between shots of some exotic

concoction and plenty of beer, we mapped out a plan for them

to come to an LSU/Bama game. Since they said they didn't

like Bama and would pull for LSU, I said, "It's on guys!"

All the other fans we met were also great. Ron from Louisville who has had tickets for forty-four years. Mike from Cincy whose daughter attends Bama 'cause she loves their football program. The Oklahoma City guys who predicted almost exactly the score. And Thomas and Audrey sitting next to us. Thomas lives in Dallas and is an assistant Attorney General with the state of Texas.

Now, about the tailgate food. Sorry to disappoint my new friends who follow the blog with a special interest in the food, but, tailgating at this game was sparse, the food real simple, and just not very memorable. NO jambalaya, gumbo, boiled shrimp, etc. etc. like at LSU. NO home cooked southern dishes like at OLE MISS or the great barbecue at TEXAS A&M. The main food was brats, more brats, hot dogs, more brats, chips & dips, runsas, which is German beef and cabbage on buns with cheese. Oh, and more brats.

The Sights

Walking across campus, it seemed so spread out I couldn't imagine how students got from class to class on time. The campus is beautiful with a green area in the middle called The Oval. The eleven-story library at one end has a study room on the top floor with a panoramic view of the campus. The Jack Nicklaus Museum is located on campus and is a well-done attraction, worth your time, and a fitting tribute to "the greatest golfer of all time." Forget it Tiger Woods fans, your ship sailed when the missus "mastered" the nine iron to the back window of his car.

The stadium was originally built in 1922, and the "Old Lady" as it is lovingly referred to, is the third largest in the US. Attendance on Saturday was 109,089. Wanna guess what's the most popular item at the concessions is? Yep, brats. What's the deal with Midwest fans and brats? Y'all need to add an alligator po-boy, or some grilled cajun sausage to the menu. But I will say the barbecue at the stadium was good and the beer was cold. That's right, unlike the SEC, which has an

alcohol ban in stadiums, at Big 10 conference games beer is

allowed. And, yes, the brats were good, but I was longing for

that alligator po-boy my Eddie and I get at LSU games.

Everyone said we had to go to a skull session. What in

the name of Johnny Deep is a skull session? So we took off to

St. John's arena to find out. There we watched both Oklahoma

and Ohio State bands perform. Then the Ohio State players and

coaches came marching in and the place went wild. Coach

Meyer of Ohio State gave a rousing speech that had even me

ready to play, and off they went. Very cool deal!

Ohio State's dotting of the "i" has been called one of

the most exciting and famous traditions in college football.

Pregame, the Ohio State band members spell out Ohio in script

on the field and a specially selected person runs up and jumps

into place where the dot should be on the i in Ohio. The person

chosen to dot the i is usually a 4th or 5th year sousaphone

player. Over the years, however, there have been celebrity

Dotters, such as Jack Nicklaus and John Glenn.

The Game

Like Bama/Florida State last week, the game started off like

two heavyweight fighters feeling each other out, and trying to

not get knocked out early . However, fireworks started in the

second half, and when the smoke cleared Oklahoma had

established itself as a strong playoff contender, and their QB

Baker Mayfield as the leading Heisman candidate. The

Buckeyes' offense looked like a turtle in molasses compared to

Oklahoma.

And I wasn't at all sure Ohio State would get their big

boy whitey-tighties on this year. It was sweet revenge for the

Sooners, and an unexpected blow for the Buckeyes. Now they

would have to run the table to make the playoffs.

FINAL SCORE: OKLAHOMA 31, OHIO STATE 16

WINNERS AND LOSERS

Winners

1) Oklahoma and Baker Mayfield. Can't emphasize enough what this win means for OK and Mayfield. Baker's game was "hell's kitchen" for OSU.

2) Clemson. Who needs DeShaun Watson? Clemson's defense may be as good or better than Bama's. Next weekend's matchup with high scoring Louisville and their returning Heisman winner Lamar Jackson will be a classic. Lamar is averaging five hundred yards per game. **CLEMSON 14, AUBURN 6**

3) Georgia. Big Win. Kirby Smart is slowly but surely turning "the tide." Georgia could be the SEC rep in the playoff.

GEORGIA 20, NOTRE DAME 19

Losers

1) Arkansas. Now what? Coach Bielema is 26-27. Offense is worse than the Swiss Army. Great knives, but, they haven't fought a battle in five hundred years. Really, Google it. Bielema's $15 million buyout has fans steaming. It would be the largest ever. The apparently unemployable Les Miles,

LSU's last coach, was over $11 million.

TCU 28, ARKANSAS 7

2) Auburn. Now what? The QB transfer Stidham was

supposed to transform the lethargic offense into, what, two

field goals? Course you can't throw when you're on your butt.

Eleven sacks? I've never heard of that.

3) Ohio State. Buckeyes crushed and made into buckeye pie.

ADDENDUM: What makes college football so wonderful...

1) Louisiana Tech fumble that caused a 3rd and ninety-three

play. You have to see it to believe it. (link) https://youtu.be/

PsK_LYWevjc

2) Penn State smack talk. Their coach said after beating bitter

in-state rival Pitt, "Last year when they beat us you thought

they won the Super Bowl. We win and it only feels like we

beat Akron."

3) Syracuse. Two years ago Syracuse fired Scott Shafer as their

head coach. Yesterday he returned as the defensive coordinator for Middle Tenn. State and beat his old boss. Good for you

Scott.

4) Baker Mayfield's only fail. Baker was magic. Baker had his

Heisman moments. But, Baker had one fail. After warming up

and playing on Ohio's field for four or five hours, he

apparently forgot it was artificial turf. Check this link: https://

youtu.be/qBL9iKC5H8c Baker ran around the field with a

huge Oklahoma flag and then proceeded to plant it at midfield.

It bounced up off the artificial turf and a temporarily confused

Baker shook it off like the Ohio State defenders he had shaken

off all day. He took off running around again.

NEXT WEEK'S GAME: CLEMSON @ LOUISVILLE

No. 2 vs. No. 14. Classic matchup, immovable object against

an irresistible force. Reigning National Champs vs. reigning

Heisman winner. Wish everyone could be with us, but, maybe

this blog will make you feel like you are there. Now this is

turning into fun!

The Jim Beam Distillery

WEEK THREE: LOUISVILLE VS. CLEMSON
PAPA JOHN'S CARDINAL STADIUM
LOUISVILLE, KENTUCKY
SEPTEMBER 16, 2017

The Hype

Super Front vs. Superman.

The defending National Champions Clemson vs. Louisville

and their reigning 2016 Heisman winner, QB Lamar Jackson.

With Clemson's stout front seven players on defense

and Louisville's Superman QB, this game is billed as the

immovable objects meets the irresistible force. Last year's

contest between these two was a classic, with Clemson winning a barn burner and going on to their second National Championship. ESPN ad hype began unabated after last Saturday's games and has built to a crescendo right up to kickoff.

Tickets, like the last two weeks, were numerous on StubHub and ranged from $150-$1000. But we bought our tickets outside the stadium for only $50 above face value and got club seats in an area that had access to an air conditioned lounge and better food.

Down on Whiskey Row and 4th Street live on Thursday and Friday nights were thousands of excited fans. Unlike last week, however, these fans didn't have that intense big cat look in their eyes. They were subdued but optimistic. I think it's due to the fact that Louisville is a newcomer to this large of a stage. Plus, Clemson fans are still wondering what life will be like without last year's departed star QB DeShaun Watson.

Before Lamar Jackson, Louisville's most famous player

was Johnny Unitas. I asked Poppa once who was the greatest

QB he ever saw. "Without a doubt it was Johnny Unitas," he

said. While playing for Memphis State in 1952, Poppa got to

witness firsthand as his team won the game, but Unitas won the

hearts of everyone present. Playing for a poor team, Unitas

threw, ran, punted, returned kicks and punts and played

defense. The myth has grown and now it's told he played the

trumpet at half, and took up tickets before the game. Unitas,

who wanted to play for Notre Dame after high school but was

told he was too skinny, went on to become one of the most

heralded NFL players of all time.

The Food

Both the restaurants around town and the tailgating food was

fabulous. Thursday night, we ate at the Sidebar on Whiskey

Row. The pimento cheese fritters and Sidebar Fondue were

excellent. The fondue had shrimp and crabmeat blended with bourbon mushrooms and a cheesy lobster cream sauce.

Before going any further, I need to explain about Bourbon in this state of Kentucky. They make everything with bourbon. I am ok with this. Like the Texas state fair where everything in the world is fried, in Kentucky, Bourbon is apparently a food group. Again, I am ok with this.

The best breakfast place in Louisville seems to be Highland Morning. The menu is diverse, the food is fresh, and the service is impeccable! As we dined on various eggs benedict creations on a sidewalk table, an old lady pushing a cart on the other side of the street began screaming. Four or five times, she yelled, "I can't believe you are eating on that dirty sidewalk." I immediately looked down to see a very clean sidewalk and thought I had been punked.

Friday night, Katie and Chuck Pence, friends in Louisville, hosted us at Porcini's Italian restaurant. In addition to being arguably the best Italian food in Louisville, it is also known for stories of one unforgettable night in particular. Rick

Pitino, Louisville's famous basketball coach, was approached

after his meal by a lady who apparently had more than tiramisu

on her mind for dessert. After everyone left, there was a

"fifteen-second encounter." That, according to Coach Pitino's

testimony. This brings a whole new meaning to "fast break."

The next chapter in the story has the woman black mailing

him. She is still in jail, and Pitino is still working through

retellings of the fifteen-second jokes. (*See link*: https://

www.google.com/amp/amp.kentucky.com/sports/spt-columns-

blogs/john-clay/article44042334.html)

Saturday for lunch we had a "Hot Brown" at the Brown

Hotel. This is a Louisville tradition that was invented in The

Roaring 20's when twelve hundred people a night danced at

Mr. Brown's hotel. After dancing, the guests were tired and

wanted to eat. He invented a dish for them that he named after

himself. It consists of turkey breast, bacon, cheese, tomatoes,

and mornay sauce. Very good and very filling.

Tailgate food: WOW! Ohio State fans need to come South and take notes. We all know how good LSU, Ole Miss, Tennessee, Mississippi State, Bama, and etc. tailgates are. Add Louisville to the list! The Honey Ginger Salmon and Marinated Tenderloin at Jimmy Anderson's caboose tailgate was awesome. There are 20 cabooses coupled on a track about a hundred and fifty yards from the stadium. Rented by individuals at $18,000 a year, they are used for tailgating during football season and any other event held in Papa John stadium. All are air-conditioned and most are very tastefully remodeled. Chris Puffer, president of the Louisville Alumni Association, invited us in to his caboose, and so did many others. All of the owners and their friends that we met were very hospitable and offered us lots of food and drink. Yes, I tried it all. The whole smoked pigs at the first caboose were great also. Tom Mueller's Caboose and Joey Craig's Caboose #6 were also gracious and everyone wanted to talk football.

Next, one more tailgate before the game. A friend,

Lenny Mellow, gave us Gary Pepper's name and number and

told us to check his crew, "The Hockey Cards." Former hockey

coaches, Gary and his friend Chris Klyczer treated us to crab

boiled cauliflower, various homemade dips, and 3-cheese

stuffed hamburgers. Not to mention Jello shots, Fireball shots,

beer, and various bourbons. I did not want to sample all those

drinks, because I'm a lightweight. But they insisted and I did

not want to be rude. Are you buying that? Anyway, they were

super hosts and we planned an LSU game with them next year.

Sunday brunch was at Proof which is an artsy foo-foo

restaurant at 21c Hotel. The hotel has been named one of the

Top 100 hotels in the world. Food was great. Especially the

thin sliced country ham. The restaurant is located on 2nd Street

in downtown Louisville and you can't miss it with it's forty-

foot gold statue of David out front. As in Michelangelo's

David, not Letterman or Bowie, 'cause you wouldn't want to

see them in this pose.

The Fans

As described above, every Clemson and Louisville fan we met was friendly and talkative. From Aaron and Maggee from Indy, to Mike Ryan who owns Caboose corner, to Mike Newton who played football at South Florida, everyone was gracious!

I do not want to forget the two ESPN guys that gave us their cards and said, "Next time call us, and we will get you back stage passes to GameDay." After I bitched at them about GameDay being in New York next week he asked, "Would you shut up if I get you back stage passes to GameDay the next time I see you?" They asked that I not reveal their names , but, a big thank you to them. Gary Pepper, who is a landscape architect, was in charge of the initial building of the waterfront project 21 years ago. According to Gary, the project turned the downtown area around. After it was finished, all of the present great developments like Whiskey Row, 4th Street Live, restaurants, hotels, and a state-of-the-art basketball arena followed. Also about this time, coach Howard Schnellenberger

came from a successful stint at Miami and transformed

Louisville football into the nationally relevant brand it is today.

Back then, too, local stores gave tickets away and

tailgaters went home when the game began. Not anymore. The

30,000 seat baseball stadium that Louisville used to play in is

now a beautiful separate 55,000 seat stadium with an

expansion set for next year that will bring seating capacity

closer to 70,000. The name of the stadium is Papa John's

Cardinal stadium and, yes, they serve pizza! Again, wearing

my LSU gear is a conversation starter everywhere I go, people

stop us and ask us "why are you here?" After telling them

about our odyssey they all want to get on the blog and come

see what an LSU night game is like.

The Sights

Kentucky produces ninety-five percent of the world's bourbon

and thirty percent of all thoroughbred horses. In 1961,

Congress declared bourbon as the official "American Spirit"

and horse-racing at Churchill Downs is a must for all visitors.

Although dressed-up gentlemen and ladies in wild hats is the

image of the Derby, any other day of racing has little or no

dress code.

The Jim Beam distillery is the worlds largest, and most

Kentuckians swell with pride when talking about it. On the

tour, which was great, there was however, swelling of a

different sort. Before the tour, I got a bourbon lemonade with a

straw. Taking in the sights outside, I didn't look at the straw as

I put it in my mouth. On my first swallow of the drink, I

realized there was something else had slipped through the

straw into my mouth. I spit it out into my palm and saw that it

was a bee! Too late! He had stung the end of my tongue and it

swelled and stayed puffed-up for the rest of the day. OUCH!

I also recommend the Louisville Slugger Museum

where you can get any size bat customized with whatever you

want engraved into the wood! It is an interactive and

informative representation of our American pastime. At night,

Whiskey Row and 4th Street Live with their various pubs and

restaurants come alive and are bustling venues late into the

night.

The Game

Every university band has a rousing pregame show, and

Louisville is no exception. The only part that I questioned were

the three male baton twirlers who danced like ballerinas and

finished with splits at midfield. They need to rethink that part.

Splits hurt! Everything else the band did measured up to most

big university bands, and they sounded great.

Just like the first two weeks, this game did not live up

to its pregame hype. Clemson took control early, and although

Louisville tied it 7-7, it was not a game after that. Lamar

Jackson's chances for winning the Heisman are about as good

as finding a DoDo bird on the 50-yard line. Baker Mayfield is

now the clear favorite for the Heisman. Looks to me at this

point like college football is Clemson, Alabama, Oklahoma,

and the seven dwarfs. No sense in beating a dead Cardinal, but

Clemson had Louisville's number in every phase of the game.

CLEMSON 47, LOUISIVILLE 21

WINNERS AND LOSERS

Winners

1) Mississippi State: The Bulldogs established themselves as

maybe the second best team in the SEC. The matchup next

week against Georgia will determine if they have truly arrived.

Many experts still consider Mullins the second best coach in

the SEC.

MISSISSIPPI STATE 37, LSU 7

2) Clemson: Alabama/Clemson III may be inevitable but

Oklahoma will have a say in that. Clemson's defense still looks

as good or better than Alabama's.

3) Oklahoma State: In what was supposed to be a competitive

game, Oklahoma State's frisbee-catching dogs and their laser accurate QB put on another beat-down against Pittsburg. Four

frisbee dogs each had over 100 yards receiving.

OKLAHOMA STATE 59, PITTSBURGH 21

Losers

1) LSU: That was so ugly! LSU's new live tiger mascot said he

wants to go back to the animal sanctuary where he came from.

If that was a fight, they would have stopped it at half-time.

MISSISSIPPI STATE 37, LSU 7

2) Tennessee's Defensive Coordinator: Never, EVER, have I

seen eleven defender's within ten yards of the line of

scrimmage at the snap of a last-second Hail Mary! Tennessee

lost this because of where their defensive backs were *not*.

Inexcusable on the coaches' part.

FLORIDA 26, TENNESSEE 20

3) Louisville and Lamar Jackson: Although the QB's chances

at a Heisman and the team's chances at a playoff are still alive,

you have to be one hell of an optimist to think either of those

will occur now.

NEXT WEEK'S GAME: TCU @ OKLAHOMA STATE

TCU, who will probably be in the Top 15, travels to Stillwater to take on Oklahoma State, who should be ranked 5 or 6, maybe 7 or 8. Whoever wins this contest will not only set itself up for a top 5 or 6 position, but will be the clear favorite to challenge Oklahoma for the Big 12 title in a playoff spot.

Parting shot: I can't say enough good things about Louisville. The city, the people, the food, and the sights were all off the charts! I recommend to anyone who has never been to Louisville, take a trip there and see for yourself.

Mr. Orange Power

WEEK FOUR: OKLAHOMA STATE VS. TCU
BOONE PICKENS STADIUM
STILLWATER, OKLAHOMA
SEPTEMBER 23, 2017

The Hype

A Cultural War Out West: The state of Texas vs. The state of
Oklahoma
IZOD vs. IFarm
FBLA (Future Business Leaders of America) vs. FFA (Future
Farmers of America)

Two cultures, two intense coaches, and two explosive offenses.

The winner becomes the favorite, against University of

Oklahoma to win the Big 12 conference and get a playoff spot

in the National Championship race. Tickets for the first 3

weeks were readily available on StubHub and at the stadium

ranging from $72-$450 a ticket.

On Friday night in Stillwater, Oklahoma, at Eskimo

Joe's, The Garage, Willie's and the other bars on the strip, fans

from both sides were ready for a shootout. They spilled onto

Washington Street and, imbued with spirits of a liquid kind, the

possibility of a rumble became apparent. After all, this is the

rough-and tumble West.

The intense anticipation of the game was also matched,

however, by the friendliest of fans. Playing second fiddle to

"Big Brother" aka Darth Vader and the University of

Oklahoma, is getting old for the Okie Fans. But like the lyrics

say in the song "Oklahoma" there is "Plen'y of heart, and

plen'y of hope." The Okies feel this may be their year.

Oklahoma State No. 6 vs. TCU No. 16. This is gonna be a real

shootout at the OK'ie Corral!

The Food

This week I was accompanied by my cuz Bobby Tonore who is

also my brother-in-law. I know that sounds so wrong , but it's

legal. As our wagon rolled in to Stillwater on Thursday night,

six hours on the trail caused saddle sores and great hunger. We

discovered a chuck wagon called The Ranchers Club. Twenty

of the wealthiest ranchers in Oklahoma contributed to build

this on-campus steakhouse, and each table has a different

painting of one of the ranches involved hanging over the table.

Great food and sizzling-good steaks. A good nights rest and us

cowpokes looked for breakfast the next morning. We found

Granny's, known for their huge homemade cinnamon rolls and

eggs-and-meats hearty breakfast food, with delicious sides.

Lunch was at Hideaway pizza across from campus.

Founded in 1957, the pizza is so good they now have sixteen

Hideaways across the state of Oklahoma. It's a campus

tradition, and a must-see for all visitors. I recommend The

Hideaway Special. This freshly made pizza dough is covered in their special sauce and then each slice is a different version off

the menu. This way you get eight different pizzas to try. My

niece Sarah Beth Gray said that I was eating too much meat on

these trips. After having steak on Thursday night, chicken-fried

steak for breakfast Friday morning, and meat on my pizza for

lunch, I decided to take her advice and go healthy for dinner.

We went to Eskimo Joe's, which is the most popular hangout

for Okie fans. ESPN and hundreds of boisterous fans were in

attendance. After carefully surveying the menu, I decided to

have applesauce and collard greens with, ah, my pulled pork.

Delicious! Known for their famous cheese fries, President

George H. Bush said Eskimo Joe's has the "best fries ever!"

Saturday morning, we had breakfast at a popular diner

called Shortcakes, which is open twenty-four hours with a

varied menu. Wanna guess their specialty? It ain't waffles or

crepes. The pancakes may have been small, but they were

cooked to perfection This place needs to franchise.

The tailgating experience was 5-star! First stop was Joe

from Oklahoma City who informed me that Oklahoma State

was God's Team. When I asked what he meant, he said it can

be found in scripture. I asked where, and Joe responded with,

"He leadeth me beside still water." Cute! His wife's cheese and

beef dip was delicious.

Next stop was the Orange Power tailgate. Jay from

Hennessey, Oklahoma, who was staying at our hotel, invited us

to his notable feast. What was once a tailgating organization

five hundred members strong, has now been reduced (by

choice) to a hundred members.

"Orange Power" is the cowpokes' slogan and nobody

exhibits its spirit like Lee Redick. Known as Mr. Orange

Power, Lee wears an Orange Jumpsuit, but not the prison

variety, with Orange Power emblazoned on the back. Lee is

known by everyone in Stillwater for not only leading the fans'

cheers during the walk-in to the stadium, he also leads the

whole stadium in cheers during the game. They say he is the

most photographed cowpoke (Oklahoma State fans) West of

Barry Sanders, their 1988 Heisman Trophy winner.

The tailgate cook Dave, "The Intoxicologist" Randy,

and the original founders of the Orange Power tailgate Dave

and Scott Sturgeon, were among the friendliest tailgaters I have

met this year. Randy is known for his homemade shots, and

insisted I try, among others, the "Pancake Shot" and the

"Purple Panty Pull Down."

The spicy grilled chicken, cherry cobbler, and other

assorted food was fabulous! Another member of Orange

Power, Rick, sold us his premium tickets for less than face

value. These seats put us five rows up on the 35-yard line.

Great people. Best tailgate this year!

The Fans

Okie fans are a very proud bunch. Considering that Oklahoma

State is rooted in agriculture, the lyrics from "Oklahoma" ring true when they sing, *"We know we belong to the land, and the*

land we belong to is grand!"

I realize some people reading this book are not

necessarily fans of football, but try to understand that this

game is more than a sport to its fans. They would tell you

football is a brightly colored thread (in school colors!) of

society that brings and binds us together. And from what I have

seen, these many threads are woven together and become more

like ropes that bind communities and families together in

unbreakable bonds that have lasted since football first began in

1869, when Princeton and Fordham played the first game.

High school football is about shutting down the

community, rolling up the sidewalks, and supporting the kids

who take the field with all your heart. That includes the band

members and cheerleaders. College football is about students,

alumni, and fans gathering to experience the color, pageantry,

and traditions of their university or college. And, there is, of

course, the massive economic impact. Some things that I have learned in the first four weeks of my odyssey seem universal.

All fans are convinced that they have the best traditions, and

they are themselves the most intense fans who ever lived.

Oklahoma State is no different. From Mr. Orange Power, to the

cowboy dressed band, to the Spirit Rider and her horse Bullet,

and the Paddle Guys, Oklahoma State is rich in tradition, if not

championship trophies. This years' Bullet is a first-timer and

apparently had a case of nerves in the first game. Upon

approaching the dark logo at mid-field, Bullet must have

thought it was a hole and threw the Spirit Rider off! Since then,

they make sure Bullet does not go past the 20-yard line.

At Eskimo Joe's, I interviewed Kurt, 13, and his

brother Carson, 8, under the watchful eye of their dad, Kyle.

Fans learn early here. Kurt said that the key to winning was to

stop TCU's run and to have no turnovers. If you want to study

fans at their best, study them before the game. Passion,

optimism, nerves, restlessness, and unbridled enthusiasm is

everywhere and all ages are caught up in the excitement. After the game, you'll find fans divided into two camps: the happy

campers, and "the bear just ate all our food" campers.

The Sights

At last week's game, I heard a radio host say that ESPN was in

New York instead of Stillwater because there was nothing to do

in Stillwater. I love my new cowboy friends, but I have got to

admit that sightseeing was in short supply. Bobby and I went to

the National College Wrestling Hall of Fame. No Hulk Hogan,

The Rock, or Gorgeous George exhibits were there. This place

was about real wrestling and Oklahoma State is the best,

winning thirty-four national titles and fifty one total. They've

also won ten in Golf, and athletic National Championships.

This makes them third in the nation, behind only UCLA and

USC. Oklahoma State's homecoming has the largest number of

alumni show up for their homecoming game, with 50,000

alumni showing up to see a football game and elaborate

exhibits all over campus that take up to three months to

construct. Boone Pickens stadium runs east and west, not north and south like every other stadium in the country. Everywhere else, when a running back goes sideways too much, the coach yells, "Go north and south, not east and west." In this stadium a coach has to be good at directions. T. Boone Pickens has donated over $500 million to the university, with most of it going to the athletic department. The football stadium is beautiful, if not huge, and Saturdays attendance set an all time record with 60,350 people in attendance. The basketball arena is more beautiful and spacious than any SEC arena except for RUPP in Kentucky.

Ok, that's it for sights. This ain't Louisville, and OKIE fans are ok with that.

On a side note, you may have seen my Breaking News post where I wrote about my opportunity to go on air with the guys at Triple Play Sports Network. During a twenty-minute interview with the radio hosts and the local newspaper sports editor, I discussed once again how I am not following

GameDay for my choice of games to attend, but that they

should be following me. When I left the station, the guys at

105.1 FM asked me to call in each week from my location and

update them on my odyssey.

The Game

Once again, the visiting team dominated the home team. Many

of the OKIE fans asked me if I was a jinx or something and

began calling me Black Cat. I am beginning to wonder if

Virginia Tech fans next week will ban me from attending. Our

seats were closer to the sideline than any where I've sat in my

sixty years of watching football. I am not exaggerating when I

say that I was so close I could hear the conversations between

the TCU players and coaches. I was within twenty-five feet of

the team. I could see beads of sweat on their foreheads!

Seemed dangerous to me. We were so close I thought they

might let me call plays. But boy did we have a close up view

Once again, the visiting team was in control from the start. Oklahoma State's QB, Mason Rudolph, had a rough day, and his Heisman stock plummeted. Although the game got interesting toward the end, I didn't believe Oklahoma State's defense couldn't stop TCU.

TCU 44, OKLAHOMA STATE 31

WINNERS AND LOSERS

Winners

1) Georgia: Now we have a contender to take on the Bull Elephant from Alabama. Beat-down doesn't begin to describe the whipping Mississippi State bulldogs took. Even Michael Vick would have cringed at this dogfight. **GEORGIA 31, MISS. STATE 3**

2) TCU: TCU's coach Gary Patterson did it again. Just when you think TCU is falling back to second-tier status, they crank it up! I saw it first hand, and it really wasn't even close. Fear the frog!

3) Penn State: In what was the most exciting game this year, Penn State scored a touchdown on the last play of the game to avoid a huge upset. It now looks like they will coast until the October 21st matchup with Michigan in Beaver Stadium.

PENN STATE 21, IOWA 19

Losers

1) Kentucky: Like groundhog day, it happened again. For thirty-one years in a row, Kentucky figured out a heartbreaking way to lose to Florida. The only thing sadder than this series is Sunday nights when my daughter has to type all of these blog posts for me.

FLORIDA 28, KENTUCKY 27

2) Oklahoma State: Their Frisbee-catching dogs this week were kenneled and muzzled.

3) GameDay: New York City? Really?! No one in New York City cares about college football, except at the handful of bars that GameDay highlighted. Look, their mission is to promote college football, and if their reasoning was truly that they

didn't want to be in Stillwater, then they should have gone to

the Georgia/Mississippi State game. The Big Apple was a BIG

MISTAKE!

Check out the best touchdown run of the day:

http://www.espn.com/video/clip?id=20794198

**NEXT WEEK'S GAME: CLEMSON vs. VIRGINIA
TECH | Blacksburg, Virginia**
The defending national champions travel to

Blacksburg, Virginia to take on the surging Virginia Tech

Hokies. The winner will position itself to take the conference

lead and maybe bigger trophies later in the year. The scenery

will be beautiful with the mountains changing colors, but,

Clemson had better be ready to play because its never easy to

win in Blacksburg. Have i told you how much fun this is yet?

Pictured Right: Hall of Fame Coach Frank Beamer

WEEK FIVE: VIRGINIA TECH VS. CLEMSON
LANE STADIUM
BLACKSBURG, VIRGINIA
SEPTEMBER 30, 2017

"WE ARE VIRGINIA TECH!"

Early on the morning of April 16, 2007, the fog slowly lifted

across the Virginia Tech campus and up the sides of the

Allegheny and Blue Ridge mountains. At 7:15 a.m. a senior,

Seung-Hui Cho, began a shooting rampage that became the

deadliest shooting by a single gunman in U.S. history. Hours

later Cho killed himself, but not before killing thirty-two

students and faculty and injuring seventeen others.

Stunned by this horrific act, students, faculty, administrators, and townsfolk bonded together over their love for their school and town. At the commencement ceremony the very next day, Nikki Giovanni, a Virginia Tech English professor and noted author, delivered an iconic speech. She began and ended her memorable speech with, "We are Virginia Tech!" Virginia Tech Hokies are a proud bunch, and students and fans take time before games to pay homage to their fallen at the "We Remember" memorial on campus.

The Hype

Tigers vs. Turkeys. This doesn't sound fair.

Ok, a Hokie is a loyal "Tech" fan. Virginia Tech used to be called Gobblers, because years ago, as the story goes, someone saw their players eating too fast. Then some student began wearing a turkey suit to games, which might have been a joke back then, but the tradition continues today. I read two articles doing research on their mascots and their names and I am still confused. I wonder if it causes an identity crisis? Kinda like

Auburn. Are you a War Eagle, Plainsman, or a Tiger? Anyway,

here the Hokies and the Gobblers celebrate GameDay with

different colored five-foot tall turkeys all around town. It looks

pretty cool, I have to say. And it must work to whip up spirit

because their teams have always played like well-coached

overachievers. And they'll need all they've got, because

Clemson, meanwhile, is still the defending National

Champions and were favored by seven points.

Of all the college towns I have been to this year, Friday

night in Blacksburg saw more fans on the street and crowding

into the various bars than any other town.

The winner of this game gets a Top 8 ranking, or better,

and sits in the "catbird's" seat in the conference.

The Food

Blacksburg should be called "Foodburg." From coastal

Mexican at Cabo Fish Taco, to fine dining at the Black Hen,

there is no shortage of options for places to get a great meal.

Ok, it's not New York or New Orleans, but I was really surprised by the number of good restaurants.

Thursday night I had pizza at The Cellar where I had a drink and great conversation with Chris Fowler from ESPN. Chris and his ESPN colleagues said they think my blog is tapping into things that fans want, but they can't get from TV coverage. Chris was a very nice guy who didn't mind sharing his free time with me.

At The Black Hen, I ate at the bar and told Andrew the bartender to feed me, meaning, "I am not picking, I trust you to pick for me." Andrew knows his food. Caesar salad, crab bisque that was as good as any in New Orleans, Filet Mignon, their Chocolate Bomb dessert, and I was done. Except for meeting people, which is a lot easier when you sit at the bar. And on this night, I had an enjoyable conversation with Jim Floyd and his girlfriend, Angie, from North Carolina. Yes guys, take heart, you can still find love at sixty.

For brunch on game day, I went to 622 North. My 622 Eggs Benedict were the best Eggs Benedict I have ever had—poached eggs, capicola ham, sun dried tomato jam, and pesto hollandaise on sourdough. Their other menu options also looked very creative and delicious.

Then it was time to head to the tailgates.

Each week the tailgates are the favorite part of my trip, as everywhere I have been the tailgaters have been warm and hospitable. Virginia Tech was no exception. From the brisket at the first tailgate, to the pulled pork and the homemade buffalo wings at the third tailgate, to the barbecue chicken at the last one, the food was fantastic. I have gained eight pounds since this odyssey began, but I decided to soldier on for my followers.

Stadium concessions were pretty much standard fare, except for one item: smoked turkey legs. They tasted great, but, look, there has got to be something wrong with eating your own mascot.

The Sights

On the ride up, I noticed the leaves beginning to change colors. The trees on the Blue Ridge mountains, at the peaks and on the sunny sides, have begun their fall metamorphosis to the beautiful colors you will see in late October. Although not a Kodak moment yet, the trees hinted of the spectacular event to come. Maybe a metaphor for the battle I am traveling to see. I hope the colors and pageantry of this week's greatest game will be just as memorable.

The beauty of Blacksburg lies in its surroundings, nestled snugly in the Shenandoah Valley between the Allegheny and Blue Ridge Mountains. The campus is beautiful with most buildings built out of an ashlar-patterned stone (Hokie Stones) quarried from university-owned land.

On campus, the botanical gardens were well done, and the memorial to the victims of the 2007 massacre is a somber, but fitting tribute. Twelve miles outside of town and half way up a mountain is Believeau Vineyards and Winery. A boutique

winery with a tasting room, they are known for their Merlot

and Riesling wines. If you are not a wine snob who thinks any

wine under $100 is not good, then you will love their wines.

To me, my favorite site on this trip was the ride up to

the winery. Valleys surrounded by mountain ranges with farms

crisscrossed by mountain streams caused me to have more than

a dozen *Wow!* moments. Absolutely gorgeous!

The Fans

I think because I was solo this week, I found myself meeting

and conversing with more fans than my other stops so far.

Virginia Tech is a land grant military school in eastern

Virginia away from the maddening crowd. Because of this,

they lean conservative and are not only proud of their school

and town but are also very proud Americans. Here you'd better

stand for the national anthem, and it is sung very loudly at the

game. I always get a little choked up during the singing of

"The Star Spangled Banner" remembering my first LSU games

as a kid with my father and how loudly the crowd sang. My

dad always told me, "Put your hand over your heart and take

your hat off, 'cause this song is the most important song you

will sing outside of church." Having served in the Army dad

was very partial to respecting the flag and the national anthem.

I talked to probably close to a hundred people this weekend

who said they would not watch another NFL game this year

because of the NFL players who would not stand for the

singing of the national anthem.

At The Cellar Thursday night, Paul and Kay Thomas

(Clemson Fans), and Dr. Randy Thomas (Hokie fan), invited

me to their tailgates. At lunch at Cabo Fish Tacos on Friday, I

met Leslie and Kevin from Ormond Beach, Florida, John

Schanz from Villanova, Pennsylvania, and Toby and his son

from New York. John said that this odyssey of mine is so cool

that he suggested I advertise it and arrange for fifteen or twenty

fans to tag along. He said, "I know there are probably

thousands of college football fans who would consider this

their ultimate college football experience." He might be on to

something.

A few days before I left for Blacksburg, Eddie sent me

a YouTube video of a guy punting in the NFL. It was a 98-yard

punt, and Eddie texted, "Is that incredible? His name is Steve

O'Neil." Then, at the Irvin and Rick from Virginia Beach

tailgate, I met a guy by the name of Steve O'Neil. I jokingly

asked, "You ever punted a football 98 yards?" He looked at me

smiling and said, "How'd you know that?" I said, "Wait,

you're the same guy?" It was him!

Statistically, the NFL told him that the record can never

be broken, only tied. Because, if you punt from your 1-yard

line to the opponents 1-yard line, it will still only be considered

a 98-yard punt. In his last year in the NFL, Steve O'Neil

punted for the Saints. I couldn't believe Eddie sent me that

video, and three days later I randomly met the guy.

At "Rip" McGinnis's tailgate, everyone was excited

and "fire-balled" up. Rip owns The Mainstreet Inn, a boutique

hotel about a block from campus that is the only downtown

hotel. After a few fireballs, I looked up and saw Frank Beamer

parking next to us. Coach Beamer is Virginia Tech's beloved

Hall of Fame retired coach, and one of the classiest guys you

will ever meet. Before I left for Blacksburg, Poppa had said, " I

know coaches who worked with Beamer and he's a classy guy.

Tell him hello for me." So I said to the coach, "Ollie Keller

said hello." Coach Beamer, with a confused look, said "

thanks tell him hello also". " Coach Beamer said he never

dreamed he would enjoy retirement so much, but that, still, he

and his wife would be "talking turkey 'til they till me under."

I got my ticket from a group of Hokie grads, Ray,

Jeremy, Yaro, and Matt. We sat on the 50-yard line and

suffered through the loss together but had a great time! When I

showed my pic with coach Beamer Ray said no way, and

argued the picture must be Photoshopped 'cause they were

locals and devoted fans and never got to meet him.

The Game

Like Texas A&M, Virginia Tech has a cadet drill band which is

called either the Tighty Whiteys or Mighty Tighties. I'm not

sure. As over fifteen hundred smartly clad cadets entered the

field, the drill reminded me of an Army/Navy game. They

formed a human tunnel for the players to enter through, right

before kickoff Then the sound system begins blaring "Enter

Sandman," an old Metallica song with a dramatic beat that is

the players' pregame entrance song. When the song starts,

everyone in the stadium begins to jump up and down. I

wondered would my knees take it. Then the players led by the

cheerleaders come charging out of the tunnel. I could literally

feel the stadium shaking. The Hokies had a regular university

band that put on a heck of a halftime show, Same song, same

dance. Five weeks in a row the visiting team has won

convincingly and the home team fans left the stadium depressed. (Not as bad as LSU fans, though. I will get to that later.)

When the Hokies score, they shoot off a cannon named "Skipper," named in honor of John F. Kennedy, who was the skipper of PT109 in WW2. The cannon is so loud and large that it has to be shot outside of the stadium.

The game itself convinced that Clemson is for real. Deshaun Watson has been replaced nicely, and the defensive front seven continue to savage opponents. The Hokies' new coach, Justin Fuente, will get them where they want to go, but it will take time.

CLEMSON 31, VIRGINIA TECH 17

WINNERS AND LOSERS

Winners

1) Troy: Let me get this straight. They got paid $985,000 to punk an SEC team that had them for Homecoming. No luck,

no bad ref calls, just beat some LSU butts. The *men* of Troy

ravaged the bayou *boys*. Helen would be proud. Achilles

wouldn't. **TROY 24, LSU 21**

2) Alabama: I have run out of superlatives. 125 points scored to

3 points from opponents in the last two weeks against SEC

competition. This is not re-load, it is re-annihilate.

ALABAMA 66, OLE MISS 3

3) Clemson: First team in history to beat three Top 15 teams

before October. QB Kelly Bryant is not only as slippery as

Jalen Hurts at Bama, but throws a better pass. Clemson's

defense is so fast opponents look like they are dragging

"Howards Rock" behind them.

Honorable Mention: Auburn, Georgia, and Washington State,

all defining wins

Losers

1) LSU: This team's troubles are deep and wide. Deep as the

Mariana Trench. Deep as a rocket science seminar. As wide as

Kim Kardashian's butt. As wide as the gap between

expectations and reality (boy does that ring true). Shock.

Disbelief. Inexcusable. These are the results from September

with this team. They may not win another game. Alabama

prediction: Bama 84, LSU 3, with Bama playing everyone on

their team including the mascot, head cheerleader, and Larry

the Dr. Pepper dude.

2) Tennessee: It is not a matter of *if,* but *when* Coach Jones will

be fired. My father-in-law, Ollie Keller, who played for the

1951 Tennessee National Championship team, fell asleep

before halftime. When he woke up in the 4th quarter, he said,

"Is Butch Jones still the coach?" Sad for me and my Tennessee

fans how far down Tennessee and LSU have gone. Maybe we

can get two-for-one counseling sessions. **GEORGIA 41,**

TENNESSEE 0

3) University of Southern California (USC). Although not out

of the playoff picture, this loss hurts. QB Sam Darnold, the

preseason Heisman pick, is struggling. He looks like a possum

in the headlights on the sidelines. He has that same blank stare

Lane Kiffin has. Speaking of personalities, could you imagine

a dinner with Les Miles (the make-no sense ex-LSU coach)

and Mike Leach (the "what did he say" Washington State

coach)? It would be like eating with two drunk Greek

philosophers speaking Latin.

NEXT WEEK'S GAME: No. 23 WEST VIRGINIA @ No. 8 TCU

Well, I see GameDay learned their lesson and decided to

follow me this week. After last week's blunder in NYC, and

me telling Chris Fowler on Thursday that I would be at TCU

next week they announced this morning that, "…after

consultation with our partners and looking ahead to the

presumed Week Six rankings, we have decided that GameDay

will follow Ed Tonore to TCU."

Onward I go…

Ed Tonore "longhorning" in the Stockyard area

**WEEK SIX: TCU VS. WEST VIRGINIA
AMON C. CARTER STADIUM
FORT WORTH, TEXAS
OCTOBER 7, 2017**

How ironic that at this precise time last week I posted a

reminder about the mass shooting in Blacksburg, Virginia, in

2007. One hour after I posted that reminder another horrific

shooting took place in Las Vegas. Our thoughts and prayers go

out to the victims and their families, and we pray this sort of

thing will stop somehow.

The Hype

Mountaineers vs. Horned Frogs
Rural vs. Urban
Coal Miners vs. Money Miners

Although the hype for this game wasn't as big as for the previous five games, it was still going to greatly influence the Big 12 conference and the national race. I've always felt that West Virginia and Boise State are two of the teams in the country that year-in and year-out get the most from their players.

West Virginia with it's small population and remote location is always at a disadvantage that they relish overcoming. TCU in Fort Worth, meanwhile, is in a populous urban setting in a state with the largest number of high school prospects in the country. Both teams can score better than Tom Cruise, but, defense often seems an afterthought. This year, however, both teams feel they finally have a tough defense coupled with traditionally strong offensive games and the combination can carry them to a championship.

And, as if the game wasn't important enough,

immediately before the kickoff the fans watched No. 3 in the

nation, Oklahoma, lose in a stunning upset to Iowa State. This

opened the door for the winner to take the lead in the

conference race and possibly earn a shot at the National

Championship playoff. LET'S GET THIS PARTY STARTED!

The Sights

This isn't Blacksburg or Stillwater. Things to do in FWD (Fort

Worth/Dallas) are too numerous to list. Six Flags, The World

Aquarium, the Arboretum & Botanical Gardens, the Stockyard

area in Fort Worth, and the long list of professional sports

teams are just a few.

Since TCU and the game are in Fort Worth, I focused

on the town known as "Cowtown" and not Dallas. The

Stockyard area is Old West and you feel like you've traveled

back in time. From the saloons and steakhouses to real

cowboys twice a day herding Longhorn cattle down the street, its historical Texas at it's best! I included a pic of a steer that

ran a block ahead of the cowboys and stopped. He looked back

like he was saying "lets go." I thought he was trained for his

part in the cattle parade until a worker next to me said, "That's

not good, he's not supposed to do that. He may charge us."

Jenny and I began looking for a tree to get behind.

Steakhouses are numerous, like Cooper's, Lonesome

Dove, and Cattlemen's where you can get calf fries, sometimes

ordered as "balls to the wall." There are plenty of saloons like

the White Elephant which has an enormous collection of

ceramic and ivory elephants and cowboy hats once belonging

to celebrities and famous locals are nailed to the ceiling and

walls. Several episodes of the television show "Texas Ranger"

were filmed in the White Elephant. Directly in front of The

White Elephant is where the Wild West's last famous gunfight

was fought in 1887 between a close friend of Wyatt Earp and a

local marksman. Apparently, the local hotshot was shot hot and

killed. Among the many other interesting saloons with decor

that will make you think Jesse James is gonna walk in at any

moment are Cavender's, and the Stockyard Hotel Saloon. And

then there's Billy Bob's, the world's largest honky-tonk or bar.

It was made famous in many movies, television series, and by

all the famous singers and musicians who have performed here.

It is soooo big it has a bull riding arena inside with real bulls,

not the Urban Cowboy-style mechanical bulls. With twenty-six

bars, 100,000 square feet, and room for six thousand cowpokes

and fillies, this barn is humongous.

I was surprised to find out that many rock groups have

also played here, not just country music stars. We saw Tanya

Tucker on Friday night, the bad girl of country music who

never married despite many flings with stars like Glenn

Campbell, Merle Haggard, and Miami Vice's Don Johnson.

And believe me, the girl still got it!

The Sundance Plaza downtown is an open air plaza

with many shops, restaurants, and bars all within a few city

blocks. The Scat Lounge is good for contemporary jazz, which is not like New Orleans jazz. If you go there, don't wear a

baseball cap. I did and was told to take it off or *scat*. But, for

some reason, cowboy hats and berets are ok. Talk about strange

bedfellows. Cowpokes and beatniks?

The Food

Lunch was at El Primo's in Mansfield, Texas. Wonderful food,

good service from Tony the manager, and great ambience. The

proprietors, Tonya and Todd, believe in all fresh ingredients,

creative dishes, and impeccable service. Must be why

celebrities are spotted in their restaurant almost weekly. Their

specialty drink is a Blue Margarita. You can order dishes like

Salmon Cancun, BJ's chili pasta, seafood burritos. Or indulge

in banana pudding with butter crunch ice cream and Amaretto.

I've mentioned only some of the creative options.

For supper we chose Del Frisco Grille for steaks. The

steaks, sides, and Jenny's prime rib stroganoff were perfect.

The tailgate food was exactly what you'd expect in Texas. Brisket, ribs, pulled pork and chicken, all cooked to perfection. Lots of sides at every stop and, of course, plenty of adult beverages.

But maybe the best eating of all was in the club section of the stadium. Food was better there than at the buffet at the Beau Rivage Casino in Biloxi. And it was free with your club ticket. There was a Cajun Corner with jambalaya, and red beans and rice. There was a Texas corner with all those described barbecue items, a dessert station with peach cobbler and apple crisp, not to mention pizza, hot dogs and hamburgers. And yes Sarah Beth, there was a veggie station!

The Fans

Overall, looking back, this was my best weekend this college football season. First, I have to give credit to Luis Rodriguez, introduced to me by a great friend, Van Meador. Luis is a '92 grad of TCU who decided to to make sure we had the best time possible. Not only did he give us recommendations of the best restaurants, bars and sights, he hosted us at a pregame party at his home two blocks from the campus, he drove us to the game in his golf cart, and Luis took us to five different tailgates! He also got us tickets in the club room, front row tickets at the concert at Billy Bob's, and introduced us to many important TCU fans and athletic administrators. If Luis isn't the mayor of Ft. Worth one day, it will be a waste of talent.

Among the host of people Luis introduced us to were Chris Del Conte, TCU's athletic director, and Jim Schlossnagle, the head baseball coach. Coach Schlossnagle and his wife were extremely nice and we enjoyed some delicious barbecue at their tailgate. He told me a great story about Skip Bertman, LSU's legendary baseball coach. Jim was an assistant coach at Tulane when Skip coached his last LSU game in a super-regional against Tulane. The winning team would go to the College World Series.

After LSU lost, Skip asked if he could say a word to the Tulane players. The Tulane coaches said why not, after all he'd won five National Championships and was set to be inducted into the NCAA Baseball Hall Of Fame. So Skip proceeded to tell the players, "The bases at the World Series are the same distance apart as here, they put their pants on just like y'all. You can and will win the world series, the state of Louisiana and LSU are behind you."

As the players went wild high five-ing each other, Skip turned to the Tulane coaches and said in a low voice so the players couldn't hear, "You won't win a game but you'll get some experience"

Next stop, we went to the Lettermen's tailgate. We met and talked to Mike Sullivan, a TCU All-American in '91. Mike is regarded as the second best guard in TCU history behind a certain gentleman named Johnny Vaught. Yep, the Hall of Fame Ole Miss coach who lead the Rebels to their best years ever.

We also met John Marsh, another '91 grad, who had eight tackles for loss and sacks against Brett Favre of the University of Southern Mississippi and Green Bay Packers fame. John, a mountain of a man, told us after his first sack to Farve he said, "You're gonna see a lot more of me slick."

At another tailgate we met Mark Merken, a Brooklyn attorney, who played basketball for the famous coach Dean Smith at North Carolina. He regaled us with stories about Coach Smith and the two Final Fours he played in.

Finally, we met Packers fans, Greg and Dan from Appleton Wisconsin who were there for the Packers/Cowboys game on Sunday. Greg told us he was in a historic spot in the Packers' Lambeau Field stadium when in 1997 Lee Roy Butler for the Packers scored a late touchdown and his momentum carried him to the first seats where he jumped into the crowd. Thus was born, the "Lambeau Leap." Greg was on the second row and grabbed Butler when he landed on the fans. Although many players from other teams copied it, the NFL later outlawed the move, but said the Packers could continue doing it being " grandfathered" in.

Once again, like every tailgate we've been to this year, all the fans welcomed us warmly and were amazed to hear about our odyssey. As we went into the stadium, Luis said, "The planners told the architects to make it the Camden Yard of college football," a reference to the Baltimore baseball stadium. They did. It's a beautiful, if not large, stadium seating 60,000. But in every detail it was done right. Extra cushiony seats, cup holders, and the best club room in football. TCU may be small with some 9,500 students enrolled, but they spared no expense on their stadium.

The Game

FINALLY, an exciting game! And the home team won!

In the first five games, the visiting team won convincingly every time. Not this time. In a nail biter, TCU won and took control of the Big 12 conference race. West

Virginia played gutsy, scoring on long plays to keep the

pressure on. But, TCU responded every time to keep the lead.

When TCU's defense was needed the most, they came up with

the plays to keep the offense in business. Lot's of games are

left, but at the halfway-point TCU fans should be excited.

The band had a pregame show outside the stadium that

was cool, and they played classic rock songs at halftime that

everyone sang to.

As the sun began to set over the western corner of the

beautiful stadium, I remarked to Jenny and Luis how lucky we

were to be here today and how gracious everyone had been.

Gonna be hard to top this trip, but there are eleven more to go.

TCU 31, WEST VIRGINIA 24

WINNERS AND LOSERS

Winners

1) MIAMI: Georgia let a great coach go, and Mark Richt is

building a powerhouse team. After whipping Miami for the last nine years, Florida State scored with a minute-and-a-half left to take the lead. But ,Miami came back and threw the albatross off their neck with a heart-stopping last second touchdown. You heard it here first, Miami is coming back to the top of college football. **MIAMI 24, FLORIDA STATE 20**

2) IOWA STATE QB JOEL LANNING: Ok get this, Lanning was the linebacker the whole game, had to come in on offense and play quarterback! Played special teams, and was photographed flying a private plane home. I'm not making that up. Rumors are he also helped Larry sell Dr. Pepper, and he played the trombone at halftime.

IOWA STATE 38, OKLAHOMA 31

No. 3) TCU: The Horned Frogs keep chugging along. Think a Horned Frog isn't a fearsome mascot? Although their colors are purple and white, you sometime see red in their logos and the goal line is red instead of white like everywhere else. This represents the fact that when a Horned Frog is threatened it actually spits blood from its eyes toward its attacker. Reminds

me of a friend's ex-wife.

TCU 31, WEST VIRGINIA 24

Losers

No. 1) OLE MISS DEFENSE: Ole Miss just opted to change

its mascot from Black Bears to Landsharks in reference to the

signature hand motion they do when they make big defensive

plays. Trouble is, the defense gave up a whopping 561 yards

and 44 points to Auburn, this after 66 points last week to

Alabama. If this keeps up, maybe they should consider

armadillos or possums cause their defense is road-kill.

AUBURN 44, OLE MISS 23

2) ARKANSAS: In what seems to be a weekly thing here,

Arkansas is back among my Losers. Coach Bielema has a

$15.4 million dollar buyout. Only a Walmart Walton, or Jerry

Jones, the billionaire Dallas Cowboys owner, could fork over

this kind of loot. Oh, that's right they are Arkansas grads.

Better hurry, the line is beginning to queue-up for replacing

coaches.

SOUTH CAROLINA 48, ARKANSAS 22

No. 3) FLORIDA: Their rabbit's foot finally wore out. After

beating Kentucky and Tennessee with luck, a missed extra

point was the difference in a 17-16 loss to last weeks No. 1

loser LSU. Their offense is worst than the Iraq army who has

50,000 ghost soldiers who get paychecks but don't even show

up for work. WAIT, didn't Florida just suspend nine players for

stealing? Wonder if they got their paychecks before they

cut'em loose? **LSU 17, FLORIDA 16**

NEXT WEEK'S GAME: AUBURN @ LSU

This is the first time in eight years there is no Top 25 matchup.

SO, the choice was TEXAS vs. OKLAHOMA, or AUBURN

vs. LSU. Since Auburn is ranked higher the Oklahoma, and

LSU is ranked higher than Texas, I picked Baton Rouge.

Whoever wins will be in control of challenging Alabama for

the West division of the SEC. And now we go to the place

where it all started for me, Tiger Stadium. I think I just heard

Big Ed say, "Hot boudin, cold couscous, come on Tigers

puush, puush, puush!" Tigers Vs Tigers! Can't wait!

Ed Tonore being interviewed by Sports Illustrated

WEEK SEVEN: LSU VS. AUBURN
TIGER STADIUM

BATON ROUGE, LOUISIANA

In November, 2015, Jonathon and Holly Perry of Monroe LA

took their six-month old son, John Clarke Perry, to the doctor

after he spiked a fever. The doctors discovered bleeding in

John Clarke's brain. After two unsuccessful surgeries , the

doctor told the parents, "I'm sorry there is nothing else we can

do. What we do need to talk about is organ donation."

The Perrys agreed, but were told infant needs for organ transplants are not common. Little did the Perrys, who were lifelong LSU fans, know that the son of diehard Auburn fans, Tucker and Amanda Boswell in Alabama, was slowly dying from a rare infection and needed a heart transplant. John Clarke did not find a donor and he passed away in late November.

Davis Boswell the two-year old son of the Boswells got good news after a hundred and fifteen days on the transplant list that a heart had been found. After a successful operation, Davis recovered.

The Boswells continued going to their Auburn games and the Perrys to their LSU games. My daughter Morgan Smith who was close friends with the Boswells had been following the transplant story of their son. Morgan also knew from our other daughter Emily Lane in Monroe about her close friends the Perry's tragedy . As you might expect, transplants are very secretive and donors are not told to whom the organs go, and neither are recipients informed of the name of the

donor.

But, Morgan put two and two together, and the rest is

history. Since Auburn and LSU both have Tiger mascots, the

story made famous by ESPN last year has come to be called

"The Heart of A Tiger" and is described as a miracle of nature

and God.

When they first met, Davis hugged John Clarke's twin

sister as though he had known her forever. Then, the two met

again on the Saturday of this game, and were escorted onto the

field to promote organ donations. As avid as we are about

sports, there is no question that some things transcend sports.

And when miracles like this happen, it's one of those moments.

You can donate to the John Clarke Perry Foundation on http://

johnclarkeperryfoundation.com and see the ESPN story on

YouTube.

The Hype

Tigers vs. Tigers

A team on the sunrise vs. a team on the sunset
A team with hope vs. a team praying to the pope

For the first time in eight years, there was no Top 25 matchup

this weekend. So I decided the No. 10 vs. No. 30 duel would

be the best of a slow weekend. The weekend turned out to be

anything but slow. Wow! Friday No. 2 Clemson and No. 8

Washington State were upset. The craziness continued

Saturday with No. 5 Washington and 3 other Top 25 teams

losing to unranked opponents.

And then there was this game.

In what can only be described as a zany, crazy series,

the LSU/Auburn series has had some doozies. There have been

more unusual moments than at a Lady Gaga concert. There

was the Earthquake Game, when LSU scored at the end to win,

and the noise was so loud it registered as an earthquake in the

LSU geological department. Or, The Barnburner, when the old

wooden gym at Auburn next to the stadium caught on fire

during the game and the flames were higher than the stadium.

Or, the Cigar Game when Coach Tuberville of Auburn had his

players come back out (on the field?) and smoke cigars after they won. Or, the Interception Game, when Auburn had one first down the entire second half but still won on three interceptions returned for touchdowns. Or, The Tuba Game when the Auburn kicker refused to move while warming up after halftime as the LSU band tried to get off the field. He made the LSU band go around him until a tuba player trucked him.

Both teams have a great dislike for Bama, but they know the path to contesting Bama is thru Tigertown. Auburn with their transfer QB are looking like a title contender and LSU has hope for a better year after last week's win at Florida. Let's throw these Tigers in a cage match, and get ready to RUMBLE IN THE JUNGLE!

The Sights

Although many fans from teams that play against LSU stay in New Orleans on their LSU trip, I'm going to keep my comments centered on Baton Rouge.

The Louisiana state capitol was built in 1932 after the infamous governor Huey Long persuaded the legislature to appropriate the funds. A champion to many and a demagogue to some, he was gunned-down, ironically, in the capitol he built. It is the tallest state capitol in the U.S. and has an observation deck on top with a marvelous view of Baton Rouge and the surrounding area. There are forty-eight front steps with the names of each one of the first forty-eight states etched into a step. Hawaii and Alaska are on the top step since they became states after the capitol was built.

I was a teenage page in the senate when one day a friend of mine, another page, threw a quarter off the deck and thirty-four stories down it went thru the roof of a car. The capitol police came for us, but when my friend confessed they fired him and let me off. Kids! You can still see the pock marks in the marble walls where the bullets gashed out hunks as Governor Long's bodyguards fired machine-guns at the perpetrator.

Within a couple blocks of the capitol is the renovated

3rd Street area. Many restaurants and shops, along with

museums, hotels, and a theater make for a lively visit. We went

to a very popular sushi restaurant, Tsunami, with its rooftop bar

overlooking the Mississippi River.

On the LSU campus the sights include Tiger Stadium,

Mike the Tiger's Habitat where LSU's live Bengal tiger mascot

resides and the Natural Science Museum. When you talk about

the iconic college football stadiums in America, the Louisiana

cathedral known as Tiger Stadium has a very prominent place.

The sixth largest college stadium by capacity, it holds 102,321.

In Louisiana, football is a religion, and Saturday is a holy day

of obligation.

One of the additions to the stadium along the way was

funded when money earmarked for dorms was diverted to

build the north end of the stadium and expand stadium capacity

by 10,000. The dorms were built into the stadium and were

used for many years, They are closed now. Also, LSU is one of only three schools still using the old style H-shaped goalpost

instead of the newer Y-style. They continue to use them so

players can maintain the tradition of running thru the uprights

onto the field.

Every survey done on live mascots finds LSU's Mike

the Tiger is the favorite. Forget dogs and horses, they're too

ordinary, and you're left with Bevo, Texas's longhorn steer;

Ralphie, Colorado's buffalo, and Mike. Mike VI lives in a $2.5

million habitat with a wading pool, climbing terrain, and

heated indoor living area. How's that for comfort, PETA?

Those other guys have doghouses or stalls.

Also on Campus is the Natural Science Museum where

among other things you can see Mike I stuffed, and hear a

recording of his original roar calling for his descendants to help

win another game. Last, but not least, of sights I'll mention is

Memorial Tower. Dedicated to all the grads who serve in the

armed forces, it has a romantic tradition that any couple who kisses at midnight under the bell tower will live happily ever after.

Baton Rouge also has three casinos, if you're feeling lucky. There's also a renowned zoo.

The Food

When I was growing up in the '50s and '60s, The Pastime Lounge was where most fans went before the game. My father grew up with the longtime manager, Joe Lipp, on Bouie Street in Hattiesburg, Mississippi, where poor Italian and Lebanese immigrants bonded together for a common cause: survival. There was also shared hope that their leap of faith in immigrating would result in a better life for themselves and their descendants. My dad and Joe never forgot those times, and I think Dad never had to pay for a pizza or a drink with Joe. The Pastime is still a fan favorite and has great po'boys and pizza.

Ok, I guess there might be some few who are uninformed, so it's time to tell you what a po'boy is. In 1929 in New Orleans, two brothers, Benny and Clovis Martin, during a streetcar workers strike, fed the workers sandwiches with meat, fried shrimp or fried oysters on French bread and jokingly referred to the workers as "poorboys." The term stuck with the sandwiches and the delicious tradition has stuck to New Orleans, and now is spread all around the South.

Dinner was at our favorite Baton Rouge restaurant, Ruffino's. Started by former Coach Gerry Dinardo, it's now owned by former LSU player Ruffin Rodrigue. This Italian eatery has a great welcoming ambience where lots of fans gather for a meal. There's a ton of energy in the place, and great creative food, and the best service around. Every home game on Friday they serve up portions of the opposing team's mascot. WHAT? We loyal LSU Tiger fans could never bite down on a slice of tiger. But since Auburn is also called War

Eagle, we were spared, and I got the War Quail, and it was delicious. All Ruffino's pasta and fish dishes are also to die for.

With Baton Rouge being close to the Gulf of Mexico, there are many seafood restaurant choices when looking for a place to chow down. Druscilla's, Mike Anderson's (a former LSU player, and great food), and George's are a just a few. The places where you can be in the company of excited fans and almost guaranteed to run into someone you know if you're an LSU fan, is either Walk-On's or the Varsity.

The Varsity is just a few feet off campus and used to be a movie theater. It's where I saw "The Graduate" back in the day. Considered a risqué film at the time, Dustin Hoffman and Anne Bancroft's actions in the movie would now be considered PG. Walk-On's was founded by two walk-on LSU basketball players who upon graduation decided to start a sports bar and grill. It became so popular, the "bistreaux & bar" is now franchised all over Louisiana.

The Fans

I know you think I'm biased, and I think so, too. But, without a

doubt, I say the best tailgating in America is at an LSU game.

Because of the diverse food and over 200,000 fans outside the

stadium, LSU is usually also actually *voted* the best tailgate in

football! I feasted on fresh soft-shell crab, boudin sausage,

slow-smoked beef tenderloin, Cajun wings, jambalaya ,

blackened pork chops, gumbo and bread pudding. Drone

surveys back-up estimates of 200,000 people tailgating at LSU

games, even though the stadium only holds 102,000. I rest my

case.

Since the '50s, every survey or article about the loudest

fans in the country have voted LSU the loudest. Georgia Tech's

famous coach Bobby Dodd said, "When we play there, it's like

leading the Christians into the roman coliseum." In 1979, the

QB for Southern California said, "We've played in the loudest

stadiums in my four years, and everywhere else is like a

daycare compared to this place." Many think the noise level

might be raised by spirits of another kind–and I won't argue the point.

In 1931, when every university's football team played in the daytime, LSU made a change that would define LSU football forever. Because of humidity and partly because of playing second fiddle to a powerhouse Tulane program that played in the daytime, LSU decided to start playing at night. A 50,000-watt WWL radio station in New Orleans began broadcasting the games at night, and it could be heard over two-thirds of the U.S. Because of the extended tailgating time before a nighttime kick-off, it seemed like the fans were whipped into a more fevered state, and once the game started, they yelled louder. Really louder. When inhibitions are lowered with adult beverages, apparently it's also noticeable in the sheer volume of yelling in the stadium.

We enjoyed talking with Dr. Albert Guillot, dentist, and Vincent Saitta, attorney, both from Lafayette. They both have tailgated in front of Memorial Tower for fifty years. That's a lot of gumbo, jambalaya and kisses with their wives under the

bell tower.

Bill and Tucker, Auburn fans, said rooting for Auburn

was like riding a rollercoaster. I said welcome to our world. At

the Honeycutt tailgate, Blaine Honeycutt said dig in and boy

did I. Charbroiled oysters, and fresh soft-shell crabs. The cook,

Tim Fontenot, said the crabs were caught that morning and

were called "whalers." Only at a certain time of the year do the

largest crabs molt and these were huge. He coated them with

some secret delicious seasoning and they were the best I've

ever had.

On to the G&G Tiger Express Social and Pleasure Club

tailgate. Shannon and Greg Klienpeter, our hosts, had great

food, great music and an interview by *Sports Illustrated*. A

cameraman walked up, and the next thing you know I'm being

interviewed by *Sports Illustrated*. Steve Ravin, the interviewer,

said it would be in their November issue, and on YouTube and

their website soon. This odyssey is taking on a life of its own. I also met a Nebraska fan, Justin, at that tailgate who said his

dream trip for college football had long been to go to a LSU

game. An Omaha resident, Justin had befriended several LSU

fans at the College World Series.

Also very interesting to me was meeting Staci and

Michael Niemeyer from Fairhope, Alabama. They had both

graduated from LSU but were academic advisors for the

Alabama football team when Michael was attending Alabama

Law School. If you've seen Last Chance U, the acclaimed

series on Netflix, you know how nerve wracking that could be.

I asked Michael why he doesn't cheer for Bama after being so

close to the program. Michael said, "Because I *was* close to the

program." Staci, an ultra-successful real estate agent, has

become a wonderful friend. We talked about the John Clarke

transplant, and turns out, Staci and Michael went though a

similar experience when Michael had a liver transplant. Tough

times bring out the best in people.

The Game

Whoa, Marie! Best game of the year! It was not decided until there was one second left. The crowd was electric even though it wasn't a night game. Most LSU fans were afraid it would be ugly for them, and after 17 minutes it was 20-0 Auburn, and ugly was most definitely in charge. Somehow, someway, the LSU players dug down deep and slowly came back to a 23-14 halftime score. Hope began to replace ugly.

The LSU defense adjusted during the half, and Auburn was completely shut out the second half. But, the question was, could the LSU freshmen (LSU was playing more freshmen than anyone in the country after six games) figure out a way to score again on an Auburn defense that had plundered every offense it had faced this year.

Early in the 4th quarter, LSU's D.J. Chark (pronounced "chark") returned a punt for a 75-yard touchdown and it was on! The LSU fans were like sharks smelling blood in the water and nobody sat down after that touchdown. Sorry Ole Miss, but the best landsharks that Saturday were in Tiger Stadium.

The defense held better than Gorilla Glue. And slowly LSU

wrestled for good field position, until they faced fourth-and-

one at the Auburn 35-yardline with 2:25 left.

I told my wife Jenny they should go for it because our

kicker had been too erratic so far this year. I just knew he was

gonna miss under this much pressure. So they didn't listen to

me, and LSU's kicker, Conner Culp, kicked it straight and true.

And then kicked another one with only 58 seconds left on the

clock! And LSU won!

And that's why I'm in the stands for these games.

That's why I was writing a blog. That's why there's this book.

As with anything in life where you face adversity, and you feel

like the underdog, but, then, you rise up and accomplish

something you weren't sure you could do, it is an amazing

thing. To do that brings a feeling of unbridled joy. That is what

I watched those LSU players do on that field against Auburn

that night. There is almost no way to describe it to readers. We really did it, is the refrain I kept hearing. Last time I saw that much explosive excitement, that kind of screaming and yelling, was on Bourbon Street after the New Orleans Saints won the Super Bowl. Now we have a new game to name in the zany LSU/Auburn series. Let's call this one "The Rally in the Valley."

For a bit of deep Cajun flavor, here's some of what longtime LSU fan Pierre Boudreaux blogged for this same game.

Pierre Boudreaux Tiger Blog: "Hooo, my sweet Camille. Jean Babtiste said best game of da year, no? Dis game go to da end an I so scared I thought I was walkin on da alligatda back. Da Tigga people dey was mo electric den Bobon Street at night. Dem Aubun Tigers went up twenda to nuttin when our Tiggas grabbed em like Troy Landry wrasslin a twelve foot alligatda. In the foth quarta dat D.J. Chark he done took dat punt all da way to Gonzales. My Tigga fans were like sharks smelling blood in da whata around Delacroix. Dat defense held

Aubun better than a nutria trap till late in da game when our

kicka he done swatted da ball thru da goalpost and we

hollowed 'laissez les bon temps rouler.' We was some happy

coonasses, no?

LSU 27, AUBURN 23

<u>**WINNERS AND LOSERS**</u>

Winners

1) US!: This was a weekend to remember. Friday, No. 6

Washington State is upset by California. Yes, the same Berkley

campus that restricts free speech, on Friday, restricted any talk

of Washington State's offense scoring 45-50 points like they

have all year. Also Syracuse had a flashback to the old days of

Jim Brown and Ernie Davis and beat No. 2 Clemson. Then on

Saturday No. 10 Auburn was burned, along with No. 5

Washington, and three other top 25 teams. This type of

unpredictability, along with all the tradition and pageantry,

makes our game the greatest game on earth.

2) OHIO STATE: After the Oklahoma loss we witnessed in Week Two, it looked like the Buckeyes would be on the outside looking in when the BCS dance begins. Not so fast, my friend! Ohio State benefited more from the Top 10 turmoil than anyone moving into No. 6. Now, with Penn State and Michigan left they can make the playoffs with a continued run.

OHIO STATE 56, NEBRASKA 14

3) MIAMI: After last week's last-second TD to beat archival Florida State, the "Cardiac Canes" followed that up with another last minute field goal to beat Georgia Tech 25-24. So, who's happier, Georgia fans with Kirby Smart leading them to No. 3 this week, or Miami fans with Mark Richt who came from Georgia to lead them to No. 8 and looks like a surging power.

Losers

1) FLORIDA: The No. 3 loser last week has now sunk (or risen) to No. 1. I know about suspensions and injuries, but come on. You're Florida. Texas A&M is like a wife shopping at

the mall unsure whether to buy something or not. Every time

they lose, they think their gonna get out from under this coach

and go shopping. I'm hearing James Franklin at Penn State is a

candidate. (I'll ask him this weekend.) Then they play good,

and put away the checkbook and go strolling around the mall

again. Anyway, Florida is on the edge of the abyss, and it's a

long way down. **TEXAS A& M 19. FLORIDA 17**

2) TENNESSEE: Hard to believe it has come to this. A once

proud team may be lucky to win even one more. Obviously,

Coach Jones is gone, only question is when. This team is worse

than the Mongolian Navy. Yep, you guessed it. They don't

have a Navy. The way the fans are deserting the stadium it

makes "Mutiny on the Bounty" look tame. **MISSOURI 50.**

TENNESSEE 17

3) ARKANSAS: Here again. Running out of cute things to say

about the Hogs. Boy, there's gonna be a lot of new coaches this

year. Arkansas was my deceased mother's team. I'm afraid to

visit her grave right now, she might come out and tell me to get my ass to Fayetteville and clean house. **ALABAMA 41, ARKANSAS 9**

NEXT WEEK'S GAME: No. 19 MICHIGAN @ No. 2 PENN STATE

This is a trip I've looked forward to all year. 110,000 fans in a white-out where they all wear white, Happy Valley, a visit to the Hershey Chocolate factory, etc. Have a great week everybody.

P.S. I've got a dilemma. Do I go to the Penn State @ Ohio State game after this weekend or somewhere we haven't been? Since I've already written about Ohio State, should I go somewhere else to give you new material? Or should I stick to our plan of the Biggest Game in the Country every weekend? I'll watch for feedback on the blog, as I let my many readers decide. I want it to be your journey just as much as mine.

Total White Out at Beaver Stadium

WEEK EIGHT: PENN STATE VS. MICHIGAN
BEAVER STADIUM
STATE COLLEGE PENNSYLVANIA

I'm sitting in the Mobile airport at 5 am on Thursday, waiting

on a flight to Harrisburg, Pennsylvania, for this week's biggest

game in the country. Michigan at Penn State pits two of the

most storied programs in college football.

While waiting on my flight, I began to reflect on life

and whatever possessed me to begin this odyssey. I'm not

exactly sure why I was in such a philosophical mood, but I'm not a morning person, so I figured at 5 am a person's brain must want to go off in search of deep and meaningful thoughts.

So, anyway...everyone has dreams and goals. Yet we get caught up in everyday life like school, work, raising kids, responsibilities, stopping by the grocery store for milk. You get the point. Before you know it, another ten years has ticked off like five minutes, and you're no closer to realizing your dream. I remember the former governor of Alabama, Bob Riley, after his second term, jumped on a Harley Davidson and hit the road for Alaska. Ok, so he had a wreck on a rainy gravel road north of Fairbanks and had to get rescued by a trucker who happened by, but he finally got to do his dream.

Most of us procrastinate and say, "next year." I did this for a long time. But then one day I said, *no more!* Life is way too short. My advice is to get up and do whatever it is you always wanted to do. Do it now. If you don't you might soon realize it's too late. If I can inspire and motivate you to realize your dream, then this adventure of mine has accomplished something great. I'm living a long-held dream of mine. My college football odyssey may not be for everybody, but for me the excitement, the people and the activities I'm experiencing are a big dose of real life, and will be forever etched in my mind.

I get to forget for awhile what CNN or Fox News is telling us about how bad things are in our country. There's another side of the coin, and I'm all over the country meeting people from all walks of life, and I can tell you this is still the greatest country ever. The warmth and kindness we have been shown from people of all races, regions, and religions have shown me how alike we all are. There's a big payoff for venturing out of our comfort zones and going after *it*, whatever that is. And, I for one, am amazed at how happy and contented I am out here on my odyssey.

The Hype

No. 16 MICHIGAN vs. No. 2 PENN STATE

*Wolverines (minus Hugh Jackman) vs. Nittany Lions (and
Saquon Barkley)*

Life after the Jerry Sandusky mess has been tough for Penn

State. If you don't know what I'm talking about, Google it. It's

too sordid to go back over and suffice it to say Penn State paid

almost $60 million in damages, faced probations, cancelled

scholarships, and suffered a terrible hit to their reputation.

But, like the Phoenix rising from the ashes, Penn State

is recovering under Coach James Franklin after he was hired

from Vanderbilt University. Franklin was hired to reinvent the

culture and brand of Penn State and after only three short years

he has made remarkable progress. His team won the Big Ten

Conference last year, but missed out on the four-team playoff

for the National Championship. But they are determined to go

the whole distance. They have not been ranked this high since

the '94 team finished at No. 2. For now, Penn State fans are

enjoying their return to the bright lights, and trying to ignore

the rumors out of Texas. Seems some Texas A&M fans are

using backdoor channels to gauge Franklin's interest in

changing from State College to College Station.

Michigan fans, however, aren't worried about their

coach, since Jim Harbaugh is a Michigan grad and is very

happy in Ann Arbor. Flamboyant and controversial, his players

love his antics and a few told me so last April. While waiting in

Atlanta to fly to Italy, we met a number of the Michigan

players who were also flying to Italy. Seems Harbaugh decided

to take his team to Italy for spring practice, and maybe turn

them into gladiators. Their spring game was probably called

the Spaghetti Bowl. One player said, "As long as we beat Ohio

State and Penn State, we will be fine." With a loss to either of

these two teams, Michigan would be eliminated from the

conference and the national picture.

If Penn State wins, they would go into next week's

game at Ohio State as the conference favorite with a great

chance to play for the National Championship . Both coaches,

have huge egos and don't like each other. Picture President

Trump and CNN, or Brad Pitt and Angelina Jolie in a cage

fight.

Our flight attendant told me her daughter was a

cheerleader at LSU for four years, but she herself graduated

from Michigan. She pleaded with me to wear Michigan's

colors at the game. This game, by the way, is Penn State's

once-a-year White Out game, where all Penn State fans wear

white. Except I will wear some purple So, yes this is a BIG

game. For this Wolverines and Lions matchup, think X-Men

wars, and you've got an idea of the intensity. Let's do this

thing!

The Sights

On Thursday we visited Hershey, Pennsylvania, the home of

Hershey's and Reese's candy factories, with Reese's Peanut

Butter Cups the number one selling candy brand in the United

States.

Milton Hershey was born in Pennsylvania in 1857, and

only went through the 4th grade. His mother and aunt talked

him into learning the art of candy-making, and from the time

he was 14 until he was 20, Milton apprenticed and traveled the

country learning from the best confectioners in his trade.

Caramel was the springboard that made him rich, and he sold

his caramel making company in the early 1890s for one million

dollars, a vast sum in that day.

During this period, Milton decided to come up with a

recipe that would allow him to mass produce milk chocolate,

since at the time it was only for the rich. Remember, this was

the beginning of the Industrial Revolution, and he decided milk

chocolate could be for everyone by applying the advances in

manufacturing to candy making. And, he built his new factory

in the dairy region of south central Pennsylvania, and the rest is

history. The town grew up around the Hershey factory and now

is a destination vacation with theme parks, numerous roller

coasters, a zoo, and museums.

The Hershey Chocolate World is a great visit with tastings, a tour, and areas where you can make your own chocolate bars. The Hershey Story and Hershey Museum are must-see, and located on Chocolate and Cocoa Avenues. The Hershey Hotel is a massive 5-star hotel on one of the highest points in town overlooking the surrounding mountains and valleys. Beautifully landscaped, it also has a spa and two renowned restaurants. At Hershey World, they have a chocolate tasting class and, yes, I was afraid I'd go into sugar shock from all the chocolates I tasted!

State College is where Penn State is located. Another land grant university like many of the others we have visited this year, it was founded in a rural area for agricultural and mechanical students. It has expanded over the years, and now includes all colleges. Penn State has the largest enrollment in Pennsylvania with around 40,000 students on the main campus. This puts it in fourth place in the country among traditional universities behind only the University of Central

Florida, 54,000; Texas A&M, 44,000; and Ohio State, 44,000.

After walking around the campus and small adjoining

town I told my wife Jenny that if I drew up a blueprint for the

most idyllic college I could imagine, this would be it. The

campus is beautiful with its rolling hills, trees with their leaves

beginning the fall colors, surrounding mountains, and a

charming adjoining town with its multitude of restaurants, bars

and shops.

We went to the Nittany Lion Shrine which you've

probably seen on TV. Why "Nittany" lion? The mountain

overlooking Penn State is Mt. Nittany, and mountain lions still

frequent the range.

Being an agricultural school in the middle of dairy

country, the college started a creamery. The Penn State

Creamery is the real deal, and to my tastes, their ice cream

would put Baskin Robbins out of business. The place is huge

with indoor and outdoor seating, many cool flavors like Peachy

Paterno and Alumni, and very long lines everyday. Its a Penn

State tradition and many superstitious grads think the team will

lose if they don't have ice cream on game day.

The All Sports Museum and the Botanical Gardens are

other must see places. Beaver Stadium is the second largest in

the U.S., and we were part of history Saturday as they broke

their all-time record with 110,823 fans dressed in white

attending the White Out game. Most of the fans in the stadium

also had white pom-poms. Surreal scene pregame with all the

white, and fireworks like I've never seen at a football game,

and the whole stadium singing one song after another. This is

big boy football! Welcome to the SEC! Oops sorry, got carried

away for a second.

I was told by a slightly inebriated grad that there is a

stone obelisk on campus that is stacked in geological order,

though, not being a geologist I'm not sure what that means. He

told me legend has it that if a virgin walks by the obelisk will

fall. And, of course it's still standing.

Quick! What is the capitol of Pennsylvania? If you answered Harrisburg, you know your state capitols. With the picturesque Susquehanna river flowing through town, Harrisburg's capitol rotunda, and the National Civil War Museum are well worth the time. Although we didn't have time to visit the Appomattox National Park, we were told it is beautiful there. The ride to Penn State was also breathtaking. Tree-covered mountains with leaves rapidly changing to fall colors, picturesque rivers running beside the roads, and beautiful Happy Valley and Juanita Valley.

The Food

Thursday night we ate at a highly recommended Italian restaurant called Gabriella's. Italian immigrants, Pietro and his wife Antonella Carcioplo, opened their ristorante fifteen years ago, and using his mother's recipes from their hometown in Sicily, it has become the number one restaurant in the state capitol. The Penne Vodka Pink Sauce with Italian ham, bacon and onions, the Lasagna, and the Veal Scaloppini were as good as any in Little Italy in New York. Leo, our waiter, said almost all the employees have been there for at least ten years and the menu hasn't changed since they opened.

On the way out, it happened again, and fortune smiled on us as it has throughout this odyssey and we met a couple sitting at the bar. He complained to the bartender that he wanted to watch the college game and not baseball because he was the biggest college football fan around. Ed Tonore, meet Bill Kohl. Bill owns Greenwood Hospitality Group, which manages high end hotels and restaurants around the country. Bill got us a suite at the Hilton, free tickets from his great friend Ken Rapp, and invited us to his tailgate. When he said there would be tomahawk steaks with a demi glaze, four pounds of fresh lump crabmeat, their version of gumbo with white wine and Yuengling Stout, Kobe burgers, wine, beer, and more, Jenny and I looked at each other and declared the blog had found this week's benefactor. "We are definitely in!" I

said.

State College Diner is great for breakfast with the usual

fare, but, their cinnamon roll "Stickies" are world famous.

Really, Google it. Lunch spots are The Corner Room, circa

1926, Herwig's Austrian Bistro, and Primanti Bro.s, where

Penn State coach Franklin does his show. The food at The

Corner Room and Primanti's was great. Friday nights on this

Odyssey have become our fine dining night and this week was

as usual, over the top.

Our NBF friend, Bill Kohl, set us up with Ted

Daugherty, the owner of The Tavern restaurant, a Penn State

stop since a bakery in the same location was converted into a

restaurant in 1916. Ted, the current owner has been serving the

best food in State College since 1981. We had the best prime

rib we've ever had. Thanks again, Ted, for the tour, and free

drinks. Also for seating us in the private Civil War Room next

to Ki-Jana Carter, Penn State's greatest running back till

Saquon Barkley, and ESPN's sideline reporter Maria Taylor,

who escorted KI-Jana to the GameDay set as the guest picker.

After hearing the menu at Bill Kohn's tailgate we

decided why go anywhere else. I know this broke with our

tradition of hitting many tailgates, but, between the

unbelievable food and the wonderful company, I just sat in a

chair and said, "Hell no I won't go." With the steaks, gumbo,

lump crabmeat sautéed in wine and butter, the Kobe burgers,

three kinds of sausages, huge grilled shrimp, you wouldn't

have left either! Bill, Ken, Steve, Eddie, and especially, Norb,

where gracious and generous hosts. They all are planning an

LSU trip next year when I will reciprocate their generosity.

Penn State is all about family and hospitality and it shines

through everywhere.

The nightlife in State College is what you'd think it

would be in a college town. Rathskeller, Zenos, Local

Whiskey, and Pickles were each packed with waiting lines of a hundred and more. Haven't seen lines that long since my last summer visit to Disney World.

The Fans

An old fraternity brother of mine, John Beca, introduced me to his cousin, Leo, who we hooked up with on Saturday and had drinks and pub food. His family was all friendly and fun folks to talk to. Stephanie, his daughter a family physician working for Penn State, said, "If Barkley goes off, we win." Son, Mike added, "The key is our defense." And Leo said, "Special teams will win for us."

Leo and NBF Bill explained the *"We are Penn State"* saying. In the 1948 Cotton Bowl, Penn State attempted to check in to its hotel when the manager said, "Your black quarterback can't stay cause blacks aren't allowed." Team captain Steve Suhey responded, "It's all of us or none, 'cause we are Penn State." This is the family and loyalty I see permeating the whole Nittany Nation.

Another great tailgater was Steve Malinowski of New York. Steve, who is in the stage production business, has an inside track for Broadway tickets. Remember Steve, you promised March tickets for Hamilton. You the man! Also interesting, were Eddie and Bill at our tailgate. On a parenthetical note, I have no idea why so many people this year don't want their last names in this blog. Do their wives not know where they are? Are they in the witness protection program? FBI's most wanted list? Anyway, Eddie and Bill, best friends who were also each others best man in their weddings, have for twenty-four years had a tradition of wearing a special hat that they got at a bowl game some years back. Whichever guy's team wins gets the hat for a year. Bill, a Michigan man, and Eddie, a Penn State grad said, they will continue the tradition until one of them dies. And then it will be buried with the first to die. I added that last part, knowing they will read this and figure that's what they should do.

Norb and his wife, Cam, are delightful people who got

a Penn State blanket as a gift from their suite seats and

promptly gave it to Jenny. The blanket really came in handy

since we didn't leave the tailgate till 3 am and its was 45

degrees!

One last tailgater was Lauren Raisl, who started a

company called Tailgate Chauffeur. With investors from the

owners of Uber, and a great idea, she is trying to get the

business licensed as the Tailgate Chauffeur of the NCAA. Her

company will pick you up after the game, help take things

down, clean up and get you home. She plans on taking the

concept nationwide.

Then, there was the blonde who works for Louis

Vuitton who said I should only buy leather Louis Vuitton

purses 'cause they will last longer, and, yes, they cost twice as

much but my wife would like 'em better. Are you kidding?

Twice as much as a Louis already cost? A fabric purse is just fine. I kept Jenny away from her. All in, this was the best overall tailgate this year!

We can't leave the fans section without mentioning Nittanyville. The students camp outside the stadium in a tent city called Nittanyville for days before the game to get front row seats and get on television. And for this game, we talked to some campers who had been there since Monday. That's wanting fifteen seconds of fame too much.

The Game

After starting the year with five straight losses to the visiting team, it's now three straight home wins! Tickets were more scarce this game than any this year. Even though there were 110,823 fans in the stadium I only saw four tickets for sale and dozens and dozens of people with their fingers up. Thankfully, Ken Rapp at the tailgate gave us two tickets and thus became our second BNF!

The atmosphere was electric and this game is a prime example of why I began this Greatest Fall Of All odyssey. The weather, the campus, the traditions, the food, and the fans exceeded all of my expectations. I remember seeing a night White Out game at Penn State about five or six years ago on TV with the whole stadium singing , and thinking I've got to experience that one day. I wish you all were here to experience this.

On the third play of the game, Saquon Barkley, Penn State's Heisman hopeful, exploded for a 75-yard TD. After going up 14-0, it looked like it might be a blowout. But with 1:30 left in the half, Michigan cut the lead to 14-13. Then came what I feel was the defining moment when Penn State scored again to make it 21-13 before half. The rout had begun. The home crowd, which had the potential to be epic-loud, settled down and enjoyed the beatdown. Final 42-13, and now Penn State heads to Ohio State next week for the biggest game in the nation.

Some final notes: The student section was the largest student attendance I've ever seen. My Penn State grads told me its usually about 30,000. It covered an entire end zone and wrapped around the sidelines to the goal line. Also, the student participation was loud and sounded almost choreographed. The band's pregame show brought Penn State fans to a frenzy, highlighted by the drum major running to midfield and doing a forward flip. If he sticks the landing, tradition declares they win. If he doesn't they take away his scholarship and put in the second-string drum major. JK.

The Marching Blue Band, as they are called, are known for intricate formations that can float and re-form while moving downfield. At halftime, they performed a number of TV show theme songs with their difficult maneuvers.

Ok, concessions. Well, uh, um, yeah, alright. I was told by their fans it sucked and I'd have to say concessions were as advertised. Probably the smallest menu and the least interesting food this year. But, everything can't be perfect.

In the fourth quarter, as the Lions were chewing

Wolverine meat, the Penn State fans began chanting, "We want

Bama!" Be careful Lion fans, I've sang that song before only

to choke on it. After the game, we tailgated until 2 am with Bill

and Ken. Then on the way home I realized my phone was

missing. I knew immediately it must have fallen out of my

pocket in the stadium. Two days later, a worker cleaning up the

stadium found it, charged it up and called me. One UPS trip

later, I had it back. That was Irish luck, added to some good

old-fashioned honesty. And, speaking of the Irish, that's next

week's trip. Maybe Notre Dame Irish eyes were smiling on me

to say what a great game I'd be in for!

PENN STATE 42, MICHIGAN 13

WINNERS AND LOSERS

Winners

1) You and I. College football is our country at it's best. The

warmest and friendliest people enjoying the the best food,

traditions and pageantry of the greatest sport on earth. And, of

course, Penn State who has turned tragedy around after a time

of mourning, and has built back up their program and earned a

right, once again, to take pride and joy in their Nittany Lions.

Now comes the real test for them as Ohio State has also

regained their swagger after losing early to Oklahoma. And it

looks like they are getting better every week. So the Penn

State/Ohio State game next week will be huge.

2) Notre Dame: The Domers are "shaking down the thunder"

again. An old fashioned butt-whipping of USC is being talked

about in every Catholic Church in America today. ND is

relevant again, and they might make the four team playoff.

Time to watch Rudy and The Gipper again, and I'm headed to

South Bend this week. **NOTRE DAME 49, USC 14**

No. 3) Running backs: While QBs like Darnold at USC, Jarret

Stidham at Auburn, and J. T. Barrett at Ohio State haven't lived

up to expectations, a number of running backs are stampeding

across America. Saquon Barkley of Penn State had 262 total

yards, three TDs and a Heisman circus catch. Darius Guide of LSU had 276 yards and became the first player in SEC history to have three games of more than 250 yards in his career. Josh Adams of Notre Dame has 191 yards and three TDs in their beat-down of USC. And, Royce Freeman of Oregon had 160 yards and became Oregon's all-time leading rusher.

Losers

1) Tennessee, again. Not only did they lose to Alabama, they couldn't even cover the 35-point spread. Embarrassing is not strong enough. My father-in-law played for General Neyland at Tennessee, and I'm sure the general is hiding his eyes now. Neyland use to say "You're here to win, and if you don't, you're not here." If he were coaching this team, they wouldn't be able to play six-man football because he'd have shown most of them the door.

ALABAMA 45, TENNESSEE 7

2) Arkansas, again. In the style of my other weekly comparison s, I have to say they are worse than the Columbian Air Force.

The Columbian Air Force once had to fire all their pilots

because they were smuggling drugs instead of looking for

them. The stumbling, bumbling, Razorbacks kinda look like

they have been hanging around Pablo Escabar and El Chapo

too much. **AUBURN 52, ARKANSAS 20**

3) Whoever chose this year to change the Ole Miss mascot to

Landsharks. Landsharks were gaffed for another 40 points and

almost 600 yards. At this rate, I think guppies or goldfish might

be more appropriate. Maybe Angelfish. No, Redfish, 'cause

they're endangered and eaten a lot. **LSU 40, OLE MISS 24**

NEXT WEEK'S GAME: THE VOTES ARE IN!

Well, my readers have spoken and the final votes are in. Only

twelve percent of my readers said go to the Ohio State/Penn

State game. Coming in second place was the Georgia/Florida

game with twenty-five percent. The overwhelming majority, at

sixty-three percent, said go to Notre Dame/North Carolina

State. I think the interest in one of the most storied program in college football will also be one of the most intriguing blogs

this year. Knute Rockne, The Four Horsemen, The Gipper, Lou

Holtz, Touchdown Jesus, The Grotto, and the most famous

fight song in history are only a few things you should get to

know. And don't forget, No. 9 vs. No.14 is a very important

game. Yes, Penn State vs. Ohio State is higher ranked, but, the

Notre Dame / North Carolina State game is a de facto

elimination game and Penn State/Ohio State is not. So, away

we go to the Gold Dome, bro.

PS: I need to thank all the people who help every week to get

this blog out. It ain't easy folks. Between writing,

proofreading, posting, and arranging pics, this is much more

work than I realized. Add in the fact that everyone wants it up

Sunday when I'm traveling back home, plus this is my busy

season at work, and you can understand what I'm talking

about. Thanks to my son Eddie and his girlfriend Meagan for

proofreading, and daughter Savannah for teaching me blogging and proofreading. And last, but not least, my wife Jenny who

has supported me in this odyssey and has helped with

everything.

Horn section of the Notre Dame band playing in the rotunda beneath the gold dome.

**WEEK NINE: NOTRE DAME VS. NORTH CAROLINA
STATE
NOTRE DAME STADIUM
SOUTH BEND, INDIANA
OCTOBER 7, 2017**

At 5'6" and 160 pounds, Daniel was not very gifted

athletically. But he had big dreams. To make matters worse, he

had dyslexia when few people knew much about it, and his

teachers thought he was just mentally challenged.

But Daniel wasn't about to give up. The more that

people said he couldn't do something, the madder and more

determined he became. Growing up with thirteen brothers and

sisters in a small house, it seemed he was destined to follow his

father and spend the rest of his life working in a power plant

for meager wages. After graduating from high school, Daniel

spent two years in the Navy, and then two years working in the

power plant. He would not give up on his dream to play

college football for Notre Dame, though he didn't know how to

accomplish it. The extremely hard admissions requirements for

Notre Dame and Daniel's small size made his dream seem

almost impossible. . His whole life all he'd been told, "You

can't." But Daniel was determined and stubborn, and was

ready to do anything for the chance to try.

He applied to Notre Dame, not once or twice, but four

times. And after that fourth application, Daniel was finally

accepted. He immediately went out for the football team. Even

he was surprised that he was allowed to try out for the team as

a walk-on. Walk-ons are the ones who lineup in scrimmage on

the opposing team, and get hammered and pummeled by the

first team. It's not a pretty picture, and these young men

usually quit pretty quickly. But Daniel, otherwise known as

Rudy, did not quit, and never gave up.

Back home nobody believed he was on the team.

They'd finally believe him when he dressed out for a game.

But that didn't happen the whole first year. Finally, his senior

year a new coach, Dan Devine, realizing the sacrifices Rudy

had gone through to remain on the team year in and year out,

and learning of the heart and determination this player had

showed without complaint, allowed Daniel to dress out.

On November 8, 1975, our man Daniel, as Rudy, was

put into the game! He got to play the last three plays. On the

very last play of the game, he sacked the Georgia Tech QB.

The fans in the stadium went crazy and the noise was

deafening. It may not sound like much, but considering the

almost impossible obstacles he overcame the sack was nothing

short of a miracle when you consider Daniel plowed through

offensive linemen who outweighed him by as much as a

hundred pounds! And brought down a QB who could not out-

maneuver him.

There is a Rudy in all of us. The vast majority of

successful people in our world have stories to tell of to

overcoming adversity and huge odds, of keeping-on through

the "Can't Crowd" and all the negativity. Make a plan and

believe you can see it happen. Watch the movie and I

guarantee you'll have a lump in your throat by the end. Oh, and

by the way, with a spoiler alert, after the game Rudy was

carried off the field by his teammates making him the first

player in the long history of Notre Dame football to be lifted

up and toted off. And, only one other player has been since.

Daniel "Rudy" Ruettiger is an inspiration and role model for

all of us.

The Hype

No. 14 North Carolina State vs. No. 8 Notre Dame
The Wolfpack vs. The Fighting Irish
Canines vs. Catholics

Although the Ohio State / Penn State game is actually higher

ranked, this game is extremely important because of Notre

Dame's reputation in the college football world, and North

Carolina State having its highest ranking since 2002. Also, this

is a de facto elimination game since whoever loses will be

eliminated from any chance of making the playoff. The loser

of the Ohio State / Penn St. game, on the other hand, could still

make the playoffs.

Last year, in a driving rainstorm, North Carolina State

beat the Irish 10-3 so revenge plays a big factor. The difference

between these two teams in the history books is as wide as a

blue whale's grin. Notre Dame has more Heisman trophy

winners, consensus National Championships, All-Americans,

mystique and movies and books written about the team than

any other college football team in America.

North Carolina State, on the other hand, has never

finished higher than No. 11. Beating the Irish this Saturday

would be the biggest win in Wolfpack history. Big Ed and I

saw the LSU / Notre Dame game in1982, which LSU won

24-14. I remember sheets of ice on the stadium seats and the

aisle where your feet rested. For my father who grew up in a

devout catholic family that trip was both spiritual and

inspirational.

One of the highlights was meeting John Madden the

famous coach and TV announcer for whom the popular video

game is named. After meeting John in Geno's East, a popular

pizza place that has been named by some the number one pizza

joint in America, he sent his limo home with Pat Summerall,

another sports announcer, and said, "You guys go on, I've

made some new friends, and we're gonna talk for awhile." An

hour later we parted after chewing the fat with John. Great

guy!

Weather for the game is predicted to be in the 30s. I've

always wanted to see a snow game but it looks iffy.

The Sights

Off-campus, the Studebaker National Museum is very interesting and brings back the history of an auto brand that once challenged Ford and Chevrolet for dominance in the U.S. years ago. The Studebaker family got Bill Gates-level rich in the 1800s and their company was the largest wagon and carriage maker in the world. That story is also told in a separate building at the museum, and you can see both with one ticket.

We took a tour of the Notre Dame campus and were blown away by the excellence in every area. From the sweeping architectural beauty to the perfectly manicured landscaping to the unique traditions of the university, I can see why their motto is "God, Country and Notre Dame." There is no Greek system. No athletic dorms. They play intramural football with pads. Their marching band's horn section plays under the Gold Dome, which is the most prominent building on campus, on Friday and Saturday, while the choral group also sings at various places around campus on Friday and Saturday.

There is a glee club that sings in front of the reflecting pool, a

pool in font of the library, on football weekends. There is a

1950s Ivy League feel to this place, like time hasn't changed it

in sixty years. I was half-expecting to hear the Glenn Miller

Band and see raccoon hats at any minute!

There are separate gates into the stadium for freshmen,

sophomores, juniors, seniors, and grads. Every student,

including alumni, is guaranteed a ticket. Student life is defined

by the hall, or dormitory, they live in, remaining in the same

one for the first three years, attending special events and

playing intramural sports as a hall. Students in the hall become

your family. Athletes, Rhodes Scholars, Future CEO's of

Fortune 500 companies, everyone is lumped together in hall

life. Each hall has its own chapel, and is crowded for every

service.

Freshmen are brought to The Grotto their first week on

campus so they know they always have that place for quiet

reflection. The Grotto is an exact 1/7th replica of The Grotto of Our Lady Of Lourdes in Lourdes, France, where the Virgin Mary appeared to St. Bernadette. The Gold Dome on the main building is probably the most well-known landmark on the Notre Dame campus. It is actually gilded in gold, and the leftover powder from the process has been used in the past to make the football helmets shinier, and a small amount of the gilding is put on every diploma. In that way, every graduate can take with them a little piece of Notre Dame.

The place of worship is called the Basilica and it is a building of gothic-inspired magnificence. The painted ceilings and walls, along with the largest collection of 19th century French stained glass in the world, make it one of the most beautiful churches in America.

Oh, lets not forget Touchdown Jesus, First Down Moses, and the Immaculate Handoff. The student library has a tile mural of Jesus with arms raised, Touchdown Jesus; there is a statue of Moses pointing to the sky with one finger, First

Down Moses; and, a statue of the Virgin Mary handing baby

Jesus to Joseph, the Immaculate Handoff. Notre Dame Stadium

was first built in 1930, and was most recently renovated in

2014 when three eight-story buildings were added onto the

existing building for luxury boxes, and the Duncan Student

Activities Center. "The House That Rockne Built" holds

77,000.

I don't have enough space here to fully cover all of

Notre Dame's legends and history but I will go with one more,

The Gipper. In 1920, George Gipp, The Gipper, Notre Dame's

All-American halfback led the Irish to a win over

Northwestern and wanted to party. Like most red-blooded

young men, George wanted to celebrate despite Coach

Rockne's curfew rules. For most of his playing career, George

would sneak out, always leaving a crack in his window so he

could sneak back in. After the Northwestern game, George felt

the call of the wild again, snuck out, and headed downtown to

show the world he was All-American at other things too.

This night however, when he returned someone had

locked him out. He fell asleep at the front door of his hall, and

on this very cold night he woke up with pneumonia. Two

weeks later he was dead. Just hours before he passed away he

told Coach Rockne, "Some time Rock, when the team is up

against it, and things are going wrong and the odds are beating

the boys, ask them to go in there with all they've got and win

one for The Gipper." President Ronald Reagan, when he was

still an actor, played The Gipper in the movie, "Knute Rockne,

All American."

In 1928, eight years after Gipper died, the Irish were

playing an undefeated Army team that everyone said couldn't

be beat. Rockne roused his team with the story of what The

Gipper had said to him, and Notre Dame won 12-6.

After the campus tour, we took the tunnel tour. You can

actually walk down the tunnel the players use to go onto and

off the field. We walked out onto the back of the end zone and

took pics. It was during this tour that we began to realize how hard Notre Dame works to ensure that fans and visitors have

the most fan-friendly experience in college football.

Employees of guest services talked to us about their mission to

make our experience the best it can be, and they were so

impressed with our football odyssey they called the guest

services director to come meet us. She said to please don't use

her name (And, here we go again. I'm not an investigative

reporter for CNN!)

She said they have seventy guest services employees

and fifteen golf carts to serve the fans. *She* said if employees

don't say at least thirty times a day, "Welcome to Notre Dame.

Can I help you with anything?" then they aren't doing their

job. I have not seen anything like this at any university I've

ever been to. Hospitality at Notre Dame is taken to another

level.

The Food

I'll remind readers, Thursday and Friday nights are always

reserved for fine dining, and this weekend it was FINE!

Thursday night we ate at Tippecanoe Place restaurant.

Tippecanoe Place Mansion was owned by the Studebaker family and was first built in 1863. The massive four-story home has twenty fireplaces and forty rooms. The food is as wonderful as the house. I had Indiana Duck with drizzled raspberry sauce and basil risotto with dried cherries. Jenny had Lobster cakes and Pasta Primavera. The guys at the table next to us worked for NBC and telecast Notre Dame games and said the Rack of Lamb and Wild Mushroom Pasta were their favorites.

Lunch Thursday was at The Legends Of Notre Dame. Just two blocks from the stadium, Legends, with its immense collection of memorabilia and great lunch items with football names, is a must-stop for campus fans and visitors alike. The on-campus hotel is The Morris Inn and has two restaurants that are both popular with varied menus.

Rohr's had the best pizza dough we've ever eaten! It tasted like my grandmother's biscuits. The toppings were great, of course, but the dough and crust were something to write

home about, or post in a blog!

Friday night's place of choice was LaSalle. The food

was definitely worth it! We had the bacon and jalapeño smoked

Gouda cheese fondue served hot in a sizzling iron skillet. Next

up, was Black Buck Antelope with sautéed sweet potato hash.

Delicious! Jenny had the wood-fired Halibut with kale and

Penne sauté. Dessert was a hot molten lava cake with

homemade strawberry ice cream and blueberries. All was

delicious! Another touchdown! Definitely adding pounds on

this odyssey!

Saturday morning, we decided to see what student food

is like so we ate breakfast at one of the dining halls. I definitely

don't remember college food like this! Think of a casino buffet

on steroids.

Lunch is best at the Knights of Columbus ribeye

sandwich charity function. The KCs have been doing this at

every home game for forty-five years and all proceeds go to

local charities. Tailgating report this week will be sparse. It was an early game, 38 degrees with a strong wind, and the tailgating isn't like at some other mega universities we've been to. I was told at the bagpipe concert by numerous fans that the best tailgating was at local residences close to campus.

Although there were some tailgates around campus, and we were invited to do, we didn't go because we were so entranced by all the university activities and the hospitality of guest services and the usher staff, that we didn't get around as much as usual. We were being treated like rock stars!

The Fans

While I was waiting on my lunch at Rohr's, I walked around the lobby of the Morris Inn. I saw an older lady sitting by herself and decided to talk to her and maybe buy her lunch. She stood and said, "I'm Sally Duncan, very nice to meet you." After talking for a few minutes, she told me her deceased husband, two sons and three grandchildren either had attended or were currently attending Notre Dame. Knowing how

involved alumni are I asked her if they were involved in

campus activities. She smiled and said, "Have you heard of the

Duncan Student Activities Center?" I told her yes, that we saw

it yesterday, and I thought it was a beautiful place. Her family

had funded the center!

When I returned to my table after a nice conversation, I

Googled her to find that she owns Silver Oak winery, one of

the finest in Napa valley, Duncan Oil, Purgatory Ski Resort in

Colorado, and maybe part of the Denver Broncos. Ok, so I still

would have bought her lunch, even though she could have

bought the restaurant. She was a very sweet lady.

After the tour on Thursday, we ran into Notre Dame

fans from New Orleans. They have family connections who are

grads and they come to at least one game every year. Chris and

Eileen Lusich love crawfish, Louisiana, and Notre Dame. Back

in the 1800s and early 1900s many catholic immigrants came

into the U.S.. The Irish, Italians, and Lebanese were like other immigrants exposed to ridicule and prejudice. Many Irish

chose to send their kids to "that small safe school in Indiana"

where they knew their kids would get a good education in a

spiritual environment. Today, just like back then, when you

step foot on campus you immediately feel the spirit, charm and

family that is Notre Dame.

Once, in the 1920s when Notre Dame beat an opponent,

the Detroit newspaper called them the Fighting Irish as a slur.

Rockne and his boys decided to embrace the phrase since many

on the team were Irish, and they took it to mean they were

scrappy.

Many wonder why the Irish never joined a conference

thinking the school thought it was too good for that. But it

wasn't by choice in the beginning. Many of the surrounding

schools didn't want to play a catholic school, so they

developed rivals like Army, Navy, Boston College and

Southern California. Now any conference would give them a

signing bonus to join them. Notre Dame is in the Atlantic

Coast Conference for sports other than football, and agreed to

play some of the ACC's teams every year for allowing them to

remain independent in football.

After breakfast on Saturday, we were walking across

campus when we were immediately met by a guest service man

on a golf cart. As usual, I was wearing my LSU gear and Mr.

Golf Cart Man asked, "Are you Ed the blogger?" I said I was

and how'd he know that? He said, "We had a meeting this

morning, and our boss said to look out for a guy in LSU gear

and take good care of him. You're famous." I didn't know what

to say. He told us to hop on, and asked us where we wanted to

go. So he took us to the main building where there was a

bagpipe performance inside in the rotunda under the dome.

Fascinating how rich and full bagpipes sound, especially in the

acoustically perfect rotunda.

Probably the most inspiring moment on this trip for me

was Trumpets Under The Dome, there in the same rotunda.

The trumpet section of the band surrounded the railing on the second and third floors and played a couple of songs, winding

up with the most famous fight song in America, of course. Fans

ten deep on all five floors got lumps in their throats soaking up

the amazing sound and singing the song.

Then the full band lined up by the front steps of the

main building and played as it marched off across campus. The

Notre Dame band is the oldest university marching band in the

U.S. Other activities that keep you entertained are the glee club

performing in front of the reflecting pool and the player walk.

Tony, from guest services, escorted us through the band

members, the crowd of players' families, and the police

officers telling them all that we were special guests. He

brought us to within feet of where the players begin their walk

across campus and into the stadium. After high-fiving most of

the players, we continued across to the tunnel where they go

into the stadium. Very cool. With Irish music blaring, we

watched as the players went through the massive crowd of

adoring fans and into the famous tunnel.

The Game

Then we met Hal Crocker. Hal, an usher, who was a perfect example of the friendliness and hospitality Notre Dame has become known for. Hal had been an usher for only twenty-five years, which by Notre Dame standards is a rookie. Hal was outside the stadium greeting people, which is not his actual job since he's an usher inside the stadium. When we told him about our odyssey, he said, "Oh yeah, I think I've heard about you guys. How would you like to sit in my section and high-five the players after they are dressed out and heading to the field?"

Can it get any better?

Sure, Hal, what do we do? He pointed and told us to head through that gate. He went on ahead, as we bought tickets, which as usual was no problem. When we went into Hal's gate, we asked where Hal was and two different ushers asked if I was Ed the blogger? "Hal is over there waiting on you," one of them said.

We were led to our seats in the middle of the student

section, which was a new experience. I'd forgotten how much

alcohol could be snuck in and how crazy students can get. But

it was a blast! Occasionally Hal, or another usher, would come

up to ask if we needed any food or drinks. They'd ask were we

having a good experience, just taking good care of us. When

we left Hal and his boss, Ray, said they wanted to come visit us

in Louisiana, and to stay connected. Then Hal gave me a

replica of the 1988 Notre Dame.National Championship ring.

Weeks later he sent me replicas of LSU's 2003 National

Championship ring, and Alabama's 2009 Alabama ring. We're

gonna make sure Hal comes down to an LSU night game so we

can return the immense hospitality shown us at Notre Dame.

After dressing out, the players come out in the middle

of the student section about twenty rows up, and wade thru the

students to the field. They must've known we were Hal's

guests because they high-fived us, and only about five other

fans in our special spot.

The North Carolina State fans we talked to said this

was their year and they seemed confident. The game started off

looking like it would be competitive, with North Carolina State

blocking a punt for a TD and going up 7-0. But the Irish only

took three plays to tie it up. If Josh Adams, the Irish's All-

American running back wasn't in the Heisman picture, he sure

is now! Last week against USC he ran for 190 yards, and this

week, 203 yards. With Saquon Barkley having a sub-par game

against Ohio State, Josh is catching up with Saquon in mock

polls.

Although the game was still within reach at halftime,

North Carolina State looked like a swimmer treading water,

and about to give out.

I said at the beginning of this book that I've always

wanted to see a game in the snow. Thursday before game day

they predicted rain and possible snow, but as we filed into the stadium they said no chance of snow and probably no rain. As

the Irish began to run away with the game late in the fourth

quarter, we said our goodbyes to Hal, and Ray, and the students

we'd met around us. I stopped to take one last look at the

venerable stadium, and as I looked up, squinting my eyes,

putting my hand up to shield the lights, I saw it. Snowflakes!

It had begun to snow, and as the small snowflakes floated all

around us, I smiled.

I walked away thinking about my father, and the aunts

and uncles who were children of Catholic immigrants and grew

up feeling the pull of that special school known as Notre

Dame. How I wished they could have been with me on this

trip to see how this school has kept the magic and mystique

they dreamed about and have worked hard to make it grow into

an even stronger tradition. As I left the stadium, I could hear

the fans and players singing the Alma Mater, and the band

playing that famous fight song one last time. I thought, I might

never get to come back here, because who knows what God

has in store for you, but if I do Hal told me, "Those seats will always be yours Ed. If you come back, call us and we will make sure you're taken care of." **FINAL SCORE: NOTRE DAME 35, NORTH CAROLINA STATE 14**

WINNERS AND LOSERS

Winners

No. 1) Notre Dame: This has to be the friendliest and most hospitable university I've ever been to. Yes, all the fans we have met and hosts who have taken us under their wings this year have been unbelievable, no mistake about that. But as far as the universities we have visited, this place is very special. Then, of course there's the matter of thrashing another worthy opponent and gaining more momentum at the right time for a run at the playoffs. Go Irish!

No. 2) Ohio State: What a game! Like a heavyweight fight where one boxer is on the ropes and looks about to lose, but reaches down deep and finds something, weathers the storm, regains his composure and fights back to win the match, this

was the stuff of legends. Now, with TCU losing, it looks like

Alabama and Georgia are the only two powerhouses left. I

know that Ohio State can come back, and Wisconsin is

undefeated, though they haven't played anyone to brag about.

Seems like they've played sisters of the poor five times in a

row.

OHIO STATE 39, PENN STATE 38

No. 3) Iowa State: This team is hotter than Salma Hayek

dancing on a waffle iron. First they beat Oklahoma, dropping

them from the ranks of the unbeaten, and now they knock off

TCU for the Horned Frogs first loss. They are now 6-2, and in

control of the Big 12 race. Their defensive coordinator is

having a highlight year and may be in line for a head coaching

job after this year. See Losers No. 2.

IOWA STATE 14, TCU 7

Losers

No. 1) Florida: Not only were Florida fans sure they'd lose, they wore shirts saying Georgia would cover the 14.5 point spread Georgia was favored by. Now we hear Florida administrators are trying to fire Jim McIlwain for cause, so they don't have to pay him his $12.9 million buyout if they fire him. Their reasoning: McIlwain said in a press conference that he and his family had some threats, but when pressed wouldn't discuss it. Florida says he made the whole story up, so they can punt him for cause. I can get my law license back, Coach, and represent you. We'll own Gatorade by next year! **GEORGIA 42, FLORIDA 7**

No. 2) The SEC coaches: We may see as many as six or seven SEC coaches replaced this year. The buyouts may approach $100 million. Think of what we could do with that much money. Cure a disease. World peace. Shutdown cable news. Oh, sorry, those three things are synonymous.

No. 3) Ole Miss: As an LSU fan, I never get tired of this. Ahead 31-7 and they lose? Choke job bigger than the Falcons in the last Super Bowl. Landsharks? I've never seen sharks

without teeth. Don't worry Ole Miss fans, if LSU loses the rest

of their games, they will be back on this board ahead of y'all.

Congrats to Arkansas for getting off the losers board. If only

because you beat some goldfish, I mean guppies, uh,

Landsharks. **ARKANSAS 38, OLE MISS 37**

NEXT WEEK'S GAME: No. 19 LSU @ No. 1 ALABAMA

This game looked like a mismatch six weeks ago, and still may

be, but LSU has righted the ship, winning three conference

games. Plus, they now have everyone healthy who missed the

two games they lost. Bama, meanwhile, continues to steamroll

through its schedule, generally making their opponents feel

like they were run thru a meat grinder. This is the classic David

vs. Goliath game. Maybe David can sling a Guice or Chark at

'em and make it interesting! Not sure where Gameday is going,

but I decided this game last week. So if they wind up in

Tuscaloosa, then they are following us again. Have a great

week and remember— chase your dream, PLAN AND CAN!

PS: THE DUMMY LEFT HIS PHONE AGAIN

I left my phone in the hotel in South Bend, and just got it back.

Also, let me toss in this: A typical conversation between my

wife and me while I'm typing the blog.

JENNY: You misspelled that word and a comma doesn't

belong here.

ED: Jenny, you work on the content first 'cause its the most

important. Then anybody can go back and do the trivial

grammatical corrections.

JENNY: Oh, so sorry, I've never been around a REAL writer.

ED: How you getting home?

JENNY: Using our credit card for a limo twelve hundred miles

work for you?

ED: Uh, where was that misspelled word and incorrect

comma?

PPS: This adventure has been one of the greatest times of my life. The people we keep meeting and the kindness and generosity they have displayed are overwhelming, but I can say this odyssey is not for the faint of heart. The miles and hours are beginning to wear me down. I went to the doctor last week and found out I had both kidney and sinus infections. So that's why I've been feeling so weak. Also, I've almost destroyed my right knee, which was already bad from two previous operations. The miles and miles of walking around the sights and campuses and back to a car usually parked a mile away has been really hard on me. I've finally decided a knee replacement will be in order after this is over. But in the meantime, I will soldier on for you guys and the Greatest Fall of All. I told a friend this was wearing me down and he said, "Seriously? You aren't looking for sympathy are you? Do you know how many people wish they were you? Get your butt back in that car and send us our blog earlier."

From Left: Eddie Tonore (Son), Ed Tonore,
Matt Tonore (Nephew), Steve Tonore (Cousin of Ed)

WEEK TEN: ALABAMA VS. LSU
BRYANT-DENNY STADIUM
TUSCALOOSA, ALABAMA
NOVEMBER 4, 2017

The Hype

No. 19 LSU vs. No. 2 Alabama
Tigers vs. Crimson Tide
Coonasses vs. Rednecks (I realize this line is a generalization,
sort of)

Seven of the last thirteen national champions have come from

the West division of the SEC conference. Since LSU beat

Auburn three weeks ago, this game looks like it may shape up to reveal the winner of the West this year, and, ultimately, a

shot to grab one of those elusive four playoff spots.

LSU would have to get help from other teams losing,

but with a win in this game, Bama would set itself up for a

showdown with Auburn, or maybe Georgia, for a playoff spot

in January.

There's a LOT of animosity between these two schools

and their fans, as in Hatfields-and-McCoys.com. It goes all the

way back to when Bear Bryant coached at Bama from the early

60s to to the early 80s. Bama dominated LSU in those days.

Even so, LSU was always a threat to Bama every year, and

LSU fans were always hoping this would be the year to beat

Bama and win the conference, or even a National

Championship ring.

Then coach Bryant retired and the LSU / Bama series

became much more competitive, with LSU and Bama going

about even-steven on wins and losses for the next twenty-five

or so years. Then in 2000, a certain barely known coach from

Michigan State was hired at LSU. When the new coach came

aboard, LSU had eight losing seasons out of the previous

eleven years. Five years later that coach left LSU for the NFL,

but not before winning two conference championships and one

National Championship. His name was Nick Saban, and Coach

Saban could have won the race for governor of Louisiana, even

after he went to the NFL.

But then the unthinkable happened. After vehemently

denying rumors of his departure, Saban abruptly left the NFL

and went to, you guessed it, LSU's bitter rival Alabama. LSU's

coach, Les Miles, got the better of Saban during his first five

years in Tuscaloosa, but then the "tide" turned, and now LSU

can't seem to put one in the W-column against Bama.

And, yes, Nick Saban will go down as the greatest

college football coach ever. Sorry, Bear, but its true. And LSU

fans still have the greatest respect for Saban, but when he took

the helm at Bama, our longtime bitter rival, that was bad.

Imagine if Bear had coached Bama for five or six years, and then took a coaching job at Auburn.

There is also a large cultural divide between the fans. LSU fans are Cajun Catholics (mostly), who eat gumbo, jambalaya, and crawfish. Bama fans are working rural Protestants (mostly), who eat meat and potatoes.

In this game, Bama is favored by 21 points, which is the largest spread in thirty years, so an LSU upset would be huge. Any long-standing rivalry game can upset predictions , so Bama had better bring their "A" game, or they could be on the outside looking in come the playoffs. Bettors and the guys on GameDay say there is a thing known as the LSU / Bama Effect. Every year, neither LSU nor Bama plays well the next game following their annual rivalry because they mentally and physically beat each other up so badly. Down here, it's called an Old Fashioned Southern Slobber Knocker.

This week, I'm accompanied by my son, Eddie, who is a sophomore at Millsaps College, and his girlfriend, Meagan

Buchannon a junior at Ole Miss. Hopefully, my son will

someday tell his kids about the epic weekends when he and his

dad went on their Big Football Adventures, an odyssey all over

the country, and the experience will be as memorable for him

as those my father and I had. Also, on this trip is my cousin,

Steve Tonore, and his son, Matt.

So strap it on, tee it up, and get ready for a war!

The Sights

Let's not forget that this Bryant-Denny stadium is the same

stadium where Big Ed got his revenge twenty years ago. After

losing to Bama in Baton Rouge in the last game he attended,

and passing away in 1997, my friends and I watched LSU whip

Bama two months later right here at this stadium.

When Trip Advisor says the Federal Building is among

the top ten things to do in Tuscaloosa, you gotta wonder what

the other nine are. As usual, the stadium here is listed No. 1, as

it is at a lot of other university cities, but there are a few interesting sights to see, some of which I have seen before, and can highly recommend. The Paul W. Bryant Museum is a must-see, and shows the progression of Alabama and Southern football through the years. It is loaded with memorabilia and somewhat interactive.

Also, on campus is the Walk of Champions at the north end of the stadium. On the west side of that wide walkway are the statues of Bama's most famous coaches, Yes, little Nicky Saban is already there. Embedded on the walk, like on the Hollywood Walk of Fame, are plaques listing Bama's National Championships to immortalize the teams' accomplishments.

The Tuscaloosa Amphitheater on the banks of the Black Warrior River hosts many concerts and plays, and the Mercedes Benz Visitor Center and factory tour outside Tuscaloosa is interesting and good for passing some time. That's about it. Birmingham, of course, is only forty-five minutes away and offers many more attractions.

One last thought about the campus: the sorority houses.

They were the biggest, most opulent I've seen anywhere.

Think, Gone With The Wind's mansion, Tara, on steroids and

you're still not close. My cousin, Steve, said the coeds were the

most beautiful he'd ever seen. Yes, I threw him under the bus.

The Food

In 1958, John "Big Daddy" Bishop woke up from a restless

night after having a dream he couldn't shake, of a business he

should start, and he felt that a higher spirit told him to pursue

this course of action. So Big Daddy Bishop began cooking,

opening a barbecue restaurant, and he called it Dreamland.

Fifty-nine years later, even after being sold to a holding

company, their ribs are still the best I've ever had, BY FAR!

Although I have one picky cousin who says Dreamland's ribs

are terrible, every other person I've ever taken there has agreed

with me. I won't mention Bobby's name, oops, sorry cuz.

Rama Jama is Bama's version of The Varsity in Atlanta and Athens, Georgia, with good burgers, sandwiches, etc. and is directly across from the stadium. It is apparently also known for its biscuits, as multiple people came in while we ordered lunch asking for leftover biscuits from breakfast.

Archibald's is another good place that takes barbecue to another level and has three locations in Tuscaloosa. The ribs, chicken, and pork are slow-smoked to perfection. For a large group, take a whole butt home. "Best butts in town" is their claim. Not according to cuz Steve. Oops, under the bus again.

The first tailgate we stopped for was the Kimble hangout. Coach Danny Kimble and his crew, including his best bud Jay doing the cooking, have been there for eight years. Since they were playing LSU, the menu for this soiree included gumbo and jambalaya among other Louisiana delights. Danny played for Bama and the Chicago Bears in the NFL and then coached high school and college for twenty-five years.

The next stop was the King shindig. This north

Alabama group has been tailgating in Tuscaloosa for twenty

years. Turns out they know my business and they've all bought

our meat products from students who sell them as fundraising

items. And they all said their Southern Heritage fundraiser was

the best ever. The barbecue was excellent and the banana

pudding was the best I've ever had. Charlotte Bryd's version

includes homemade shortbread cookies instead of vanilla

wafers. Whoa daddy!

Then, Ron King, the big Kahuna at this tailgate,

introduced me to Coach Jeff Pugh, head football coach at East

Limestone High School, who said we might do some

fundraising business. His football team and boosters sell

strawberries for a fundraiser, and that's also a product we

provide, so maybe this trip will pay for itself.

Then, it was on to the Tailgater Guys tailgate. In the

middle of a large green area with a pretty lawn and surrounded

by giant trees known as The Quad, these folks had set up a

slice of heaven. Surrounded by only the portable white picket

fence around this tailgate, it had everything you needed. Shade,

barbecue and a big menu, chairs, a bar with a bartender,

dessert, giant flat-screen TV, and a table with Tylenol,

ibuprofen and stomach meds for the medically challenged. But

best of all Lance, Chris and all the guys provided me with a

knowledgeable discussion of college football. In many places

I've been on my travels, fans' knowledge of the game and

other teams is very limited due to their lack of exposure to

teams and traditions other than their own. They're satisfied to

think that their tradition and their team is the greatest and, of

course, to them that's so. But I'm here to say there's a big

world of college football out there and everybody's team and

its traditions has something to contribute to the big picture of

this the best game in sports. Tailgate Guys were knowledgeable

and friendly, and not overbearing like some fans. One of my

bankers, Fred from National Bank of Commerce, came in and

said, "Someone outside this tailgate told me there was a

blogger in this party." And I said, "I bet I know who that is."

It's great when you run into people you know on game day.

Thanks again, Lance, for the invite and the warm hospitality.

Concession food was average and the usual, except for

the Dreamland nachos. Like regular nachos, except with the

famous Dreamland barbecue poured over the top. Now that's

food to dream about. My son and his girlfriend promptly

wolfed down their nachos before I could even finish my

hotdog.

The Fans

Anytime a sports team gets on such a roll that people begin to

call the program a "dynasty," the fans can get a little, how shall

I say, overzealous. And it's not just Alabama fans. It's

happened throughout history, it happens anywhere, because it's

human nature. So, I guess I can excuse the Rama Jama fan

sitting next to me who jumped up and screamed on every play.

Even when his team had a 1-yard gain. Not everyone is like

that, of course, and every team has its small percentage of fans

who need to have a come-to-Jesus meeting and lighten up a

little. Or not! This is college football!

You have to understand, Bama is on a roll like I don't

think has happened in college football since Notre Dame and

Knute Rockne in the 20s. With social media, week-long sports

television, an ever-expanding population, and people's need to

escape politics and the day-to-day drudgery, and an unmatched

winning tradition, have all merged together to give Alabama a

following the likes of which I haven't seen in my lifetime. I'd

say, however it's a very small percentage of America who

watches and adores the Crimson Tide, while the rest watches

and hates them. Bama fans know this and don't care, 'cause

they know it comes with the territory. Ed Smith, a '56 grad I

met, said, "You know why we are called the Capstone, because

we're always on top."

When *Rolling Stone* magazine asked Donald Fagen and

Walter Becker of the rock group Steely Dan what they meant

by their line, *Crimson Tide and Deacon Blues* in the song

"Deacon Blues" they had an interesting answer. Fagan said,

"We were working on that song and Walter asked what the

words meant. When I explained it to him he said, 'so they call

these crackers in Alabama this grandiose name of Crimson

Tide and I'm this loser so I'm Deacon Blue?' and I said, yeah,

that's it.

Fagan also said the Deacon wasn't a reference to Wake

Forest UniversityDemon Deacons, but to Deacon Jones the

NFL player, who, ironically, was definitely not a loser.

The origin of the team name Crimson Tide came from

two sources. In 1907, a sportswriter watching Bama play

Auburn in the rain and mud coined the phrase as a description

of the bloody beating the Alabama team was giving Auburn.

The mud turned the Bama players jerseys red. Then after

WW2, a returning Bama grad related how he compared the

surf overseas to his Bama team, "it was a force that just kept

pounding." The Red Elephant thing as a mascot came about in

1931 when Bama went to the Rose Bowl. The team was given trunks from the Rosenburg Trunk Company to carry their clothes in. Upon arriving in Los Angeles, a sportswriter saw the trunks with red elephant logos on them and called them the Red Elephants. Although it caught on and everyone began to use the name, it wasn't officially adopted by the University of Alabama until 1978.

The Bama band is large and very popular, called The Million Dollar Band, and performs nice pregame and halftime shows with complicated movements that must take about as much practice as the football team. They've been at it for 106 years, and it's the largest student organization on campus. Three parachuters carrying flags swooped in pregame to a roaring crowd. Same aerial drop-in as at Virginia Tech, but here the stadium is so tall and steep they had to dive-bomb in for their landing instead of the flatter approach made in Blacksburg.

The Game

Their team a 21.5-point underdog, LSU fans felt as if the Tigers had improved enough not to be that big a dog. As the game would unfold, they were correct. Although Bama seemed in control the entire game, LSU never gave up and actually out-gained Alabama. Were it not for a couple plays, specifically a multitude of barely overthrown deep passes, the Tigers could have won. But great teams find a way to win, and Bama did. The final score of 24-10 wasn't as close as the game, and LSU has a promising future considering they've played more freshman than any team in the nation, including two starters on the offensive line. In the end, the pachyderms ran over the Bengals but not without the tiger leaving the Red Elephant severely wounded. Bama had several players suffer injuries during the game and lost two more linebackers for the season.

This win keeps Bama on a collision course with Georgia to

play for the SEC championship, but Auburn will have

something to say about that.

FINAL SCORE: ALABAMA 24, LSU 10

WINNERS AND LOSERS

Winners

1) Baker Mayfield: On the road at rival Oklahoma State, the

QB for Oklahoma once again showed he is better on the road

than Willie Nelson. He is 13-0 in big road games, and has

scored 55 career touchdowns. The Heisman is now his to lose.

You win the trophy in November and his November has started

with a bang. The other contenders had average to poor

showings this week, and are now in Bakers rearview mirror.

"Baker" is the "cake boss" of college football now!

OKLAHOMA 62, OKLAHOMA STATE 52

2) Penn State coach James Franklin: Yes, I know, they lost.

But, what happened after the game is what our society needs

more of. When he saw some disappointed Penn State players

heading to the locker room without shaking the hand of their

opponents, he literally ran them down and said, "Go back and

shake their hand, now!" High road or low road, its always been

up to the individual, and it helps when young men on a football

team take the high road when the coach isn't looking.

3) Iowa: After losing to Penn State earlier this year on the last

play of the game, Iowa proved once again it is a formidable

home team, knocking off No. 3 Ohio State. Not only did they

win, they treated the Buckeyes like a radioactive brother-in-

law. Get out and don't come back! The Hawkeyes of Iowa are

4-1 against Top 5 teams since 2008 and became the first team

to hang 50 or more points on Ohio State since 1994. **IOWA 55,**

OHIO STATE 24

Losers

1) The Big Ten: No. 3 Ohio State got taken to the woodshed.

Penn State was beaten for the second week in a row and both

were eliminated from the playoffs. Wisconsin is the Big Ten's only playoff hope, which might work out for them since they are still playing nobody. This week they played William & Mary and William was hurt.

2) Texas A&M: Chinese torture isn't this bad. How much longer are Aggie Fans gonna have to twist in the wind? Aggie fans are knowledgeable and proud and apparently more patient than Job. Someone said, "Patience is the companion of wisdom." And I say, hard headedness is the companion of last place in the SEC." **AUBURN 42, TEXAS A&M 27**

3) Rat Poison: After the 27-19 win against Texas A&M last week, Coach Saban said his Alabama team wasn't playing up to his standards due to the adulation the media was feeding his players. He said, "It's like rat poison y'all are feeding my players." Ever since Saban's statement, rat traps are flying off the shelves and poison isn't moving. Such is the influence of this coach. Ramik and Tomcat, the leading manufactures of rat poison have seen their stock plunge and are talking Chapter 13 bankruptcy. Mickey and Minnie Mouse sent a thank you note

to Saban and promise they'll attend the next game. Saban

replied, "No thanks, elephants run from mice."

NEXT WEEK'S GAME: No. 1 GEORGIA @ No. 10 AUBURN

Now it gets interesting. Georgia has played like the No. 1 or

No. 2 team all year, and now they have to play in a very hostile

environment against an Auburn team that is hotter than a blister

bug in a pepper patch. GameDay heard two weeks ago I was

going there, so they began their plans to follow me and to not

go to the Miami/Notre Dame game. If anyone can challenge

Alabama, it's Georgia or Auburn, or maybe both. This rivalry

has had some historic games, which I will detail in next week's

blog. Big Ed used to say, "Why do so many teams have a Tiger

mascot? LSU was first before these other Johnny come lately

guys." Sorry Dad, but I think Princeton were the Tigers before

LSU fans were making gumbo and hunting alligators. Until

next weekend, have a great week and remember, don't let

people tell your children they are doing great in school or

athletics because it might be "rat poison."

Rushing the field: Find Ed

**WEEK ELEVEN: AUBURN VS. GEORGIA
JORDAN-HARE STADIUM
AUBURN, ALABAMA**

Winters in northern Alabama are biting and bone-chilling, especially to a child living in a one bedroom house with nine brothers and sisters. The wind comes whistling through the cracks and the outhouse is too far away for quick nighttime visits. You are more likely to hold it. Food is scarce even when your single mother is working two jobs.

When a child grows up in this environment, going to bed cold and hungry, and with no father present, a lot of anger is likely to build up. And anger is what drove little Vincent.

Bullying and stealing became a way of life for him. So did

mayhem. He broke, destroyed, and defaced so many things that

no one knew what to do with Vincent. By the time he reached

high school he had grown into a very powerful, muscular, and

mean young man. Then he met his mentor, Coach Atchinson,

and his life turned around.

Coach Atchinson was his track coach and later his

football coach. He was the missing piece of Vincent's puzzle

and his presence filled a critical void. With help from his

coach, by the time Vincent graduated he had learned to channel

his anger into superior athletic skills on the playing field and

he was offered scholarships from every major college in the

country. And, most important to Vincent, he knew that he had

become someone his mother was proud of. Years later, Vincent

said his mother was the strongest person he had ever known

and he gave her credit for serving as both father and mother to

him.

Vincent Jackson, otherwise known as "Bo," has been

called by many people the greatest athlete ever, an all-star in

football, and baseball, who ran the 40-yard dash in 4.13

seconds, and who won the Heisman Trophy. Bo Jackson, now a

father with three children, says his proudest accomplishment is

not being a sports legend, it is being a standup father. We may

not have grown up poor, hungry and angry like Bo, but most of

us have had someone who was a mentor and showed us

patience, guidance and unconditional love. Whether it was

your parents, a teacher, pastor or coach, you credit them with

helping you to be who you are today. If you have someone

who's been there for you as a guide and mentor, please pick up

the phone now and call that person. And it it turns out they are

no longer alive, still, stop for a minute and silently thank them

for all they did.

The Hype

No. 1 Georgia vs. No. 10 Auburn

Bulldogs vs. Tigers (Plainsmen, War Eagles...make up your mind)
The oldest rivalry in the South

This is what big boy football is all about. Hide your kids, and warn your wife or your husband. This is going to be a war involving two very athletic and aggressive teams. Georgia, after so many years of being close to the mountaintop, now believes that their new coach, Kirby Smart, can lead them to the top of their game and take the team to heights their previous coaches only dreamed of.

Auburn, after close losses to No. 4 Clemson and No. 30` LSU (see Week Seven), are running on all cylinders and feel the home field advantage will propel them to a win, and into the playoff discussion. Whichever team wins will surely hear its fans yelling that cheer they should stay away from, "We want Bama!" Last time we heard that was in Week Eight when Penn State fans boasted that song, and then proceeded to choke on two losses in a row.

Tickets for this game were on Stubhub at the highest

prices of the year. Alabama Electric could power Montgomery

off the electricity in the stadium. Seriously, this could turn out

to be the most intense game this year. Strap it on, gird your

loins, and get ready for some "What?!" moments.

The Sights

I gather Auburnites (if there's not such a word, now there is)

are outdoors people. The top ten sights in and around Auburn

include Chewacla State Park, Tuskegee National Forest, Town

Creek Park, Sam Harris Park, Lake Wilmore Park, Moore's

Mill Park, and Lake Martin. Camping and hiking are popular

with the students and fans when Auburn's football team isn't

playing. Lake Martin, which is only 20-30 minutes away, has

over 750 miles of shoreline, and is the site of second homes to

many of Atlanta and Birmingham's wealthiest residents.

On the corner of Magnolia Avenue and College Street

is Toomer's Corner where Sheldon Toomer founded Toomer's

Drugs in 1896. In 1937, directly across the street from the drugstore on campus, two oak trees were planted and over the years have grown to huge size. A tradition has also grown up around the trees, and when Auburn wins a big game, fans throw toilet paper over the trees draping the branches is white. It's a victory cry known as "rolling the corner," or "rolling Toomer's."

The tradition is said to have begun when Toomer's Drugs had the only telegraph in town. After a big football win, ticker tape from the telegraph describing the results would be thrown on the two oak trees and electric lines. Yes, kids, ticker tape. Google it! There actually was a recent time when there were no phones or computers. Then as ticker tape went the way of the horse and buggy, the handiest rolls of paper were—you guessed it.

The tradition of rolling the Toomer Oaks continued until 2010 when an Alabama fan, Harvey Updike, poisoned the trees with a extremely strong herbicide, Spike 80DF, which eventually killed the 85-year old trees and iconic landmarks for Auburn. Harvey told the media he was mad that Auburn had beaten his beloved Crimson Tide and decided to get them back. See last week's game for a discussion of "overzealous fans." Maybe insane would be more appropriate.

But, then again, what would you expect from a man who named his first son Bear Bryant Updike, his first daughter Crimson Tyde, his second son Bear Updike, and then actually tried to convince his new wife to name his next daughter Ally Bama? Her response, it is reported, was priceless: "Are you crazy?"

Duh, what was your first clue, lady?

Let's not forget the family dogs named Bama, and Nicky. You can't make this stuff up!

The trees had to be cut down and were replaced with mature oaks and fans are once again back in toilet paper heaven. Before you leave Toomer's, try the chicken salad sandwich and lemonade at the drugstore.

Last, but not least, is the Southeastern Raptor Center where Auburn's live mascot, an eagle named Nova, is kept along with other raptors and where you can see demonstrations at certain times of the year. ESPN named Auburn's War Eagle flight the No. 1 SEC pregame tradition. The eagle flies from a perch atop the stadium, then around the inside of the stadium barely clearing fans at times, until it lands at midfield. Unfortunately, Nova has been diagnosed with cardiomyopathy and will not fly this year. However, a new eagle named Spirit has replaced him and is ready for wheels up this Saturday.

The battle cry "War Eagle!" came about from an event in 1892, ironically, the first Georgia/Auburn game. An old civil war soldier in the stands had a pet 30-year old eagle which broke loose and soared majestically above the field as Auburn drove relentlessly toward the winning touchdown. Auburn students and fans began chanting, "War Eagle!" and it stuck. Sadly, the original War Eagle landed at midfield and collapsed, and though he died, created a tradition that has lived on since.

The Food

Food options in the Auburn/Opelika area are much better than you'd think for a mostly rural area. As far as honing in on Auburn dining establishments, one place in particular comes to mind, Momma Goldberg's Deli, a specialty sandwich shop that opened in 1976. The original is on the edge of Auburn's campus and still operates. Momma Goldberg's is known for steamed sandwiches, but I must mention their famed nachos. They consist of regular nacho cheese Doritos topped with pepper jack cheese and jalapeños. It sounds simple, but the key is that they are steamed. Sounds crazy, but trust me, the nachos are awesome. You can try this at home but they aren't quite the same.

Other eateries in Auburn worth a mention are Hamilton's Downtown for fine dining, and Amsterdam Cafe. New to the scene for Auburn eats is Acre, and Hound, and both have good food, cocktails, and great ambiance. It was good to see the growth taking place around Auburn, and a better variety

of cuisine showing up on the restaurant scene.

I can't continue without mentioning The War Eagle

Supper Club. Although it's now out of business, it holds a

special place in the hearts of Auburn alumni, students, and

locals. At one time in its early years, it was a brothel. Later it

became a sanctuary of men's-only dining, smoking, and card

playing. Sort of like a revved-up man cave. Eventually, the

men saw the error of their ways, so to speak, and it became a

private club for both men and women. In other words Auburn

women asked, "What are you eating tonight, and where do you

think you're sleeping?" The War Eagle Supper Club's last call

was on December 31, 2015 and is now only a good memory.

Speaking of last calls, the bar called 1716 is quite the

hotspot, and named for an Auburn win over Alabama in 1972

when Auburn beat Alabama 17-16. And well, there you have it!

Rivalry at its finest when football scores become the names for local establishments. 1716 has pool tables, live music, big

screens, you get the picture.

Tailgating, like at other Southern mega universities, is

everywhere you look on game day and varying in size and

what's on the table. I had to stop at one tailgate just because of

its location one block from the stadium under a large Auburn

tent and run by Greg Ellison's group from Huntsville. It was a

huge tailgate, sprawling for acres, it seemed!

Right on the corner where the team buses turn was War

Eagle Heaven. Big screen TV, plenty of shade, chairs, and

homemade good eating. No fast food here! Everything was

made in home kitchens and was delicious. Two kinds of chili,

pulled pork, moist cornbread, numerous dips, and award-

winning desserts were everywhere. After the game, back in

War Eagle Heaven we had grilled cheese sandwiches to rival

my cousin Todd's, and s'mores over a roaring fire pit. Don't

want to forget to mention Dede's blue ribbon pound cake, and

Greg's wife Kelly's Captain Crunch Crack dessert. Gracious

and warm doesn't begin to describe Greg, Kelly, Steve,

Professor Mark Clark, and Dede and Todd. We will be back for

the Bama game and try for a few more well-placed pounds!

A good friend and retired ag (agriculture, to the

uninformed) teacher, Brian Grantham, invited us to his tailgate

where we enjoyed meeting Francis, Eric and Lavana. The

Francis Cheesy Bacon Dip was the dip of the day. Auburn fans

for forty years, Eric and Francis said Auburn could win by 3, or

get killed. Funny, but Greg at the previous tailgate said the

same thing.

Previously at 1716, we had met John, Melanie and their

son Chaz Cooksey who were Georgia fans. Hailing from

Monroe, Georgia, John is a football coach with a bond to the

Bulldogs that's stickier than Gorilla glue. John has been to 339

Georgia football games straight, home and away for over

twenty-seven years. Read that again and think about his

dedication as a fan. And I thought going to the biggest game in the country each weekend for an entire season was

monumental!

Like I said earlier, tickets were harder to find than

Colin Kaepernick on an NFL rooster. Jenny found a guy on a

bike who said he had a pair on the 45-yard line he'd let go for

$250 'cause he was in a hurry to buy Lotto tickets. O-o-o-o

kay-y-y-y-y. When we got to our seats we felt like we had won

the lottery. Turns out they were as good as advertised, and we

sat surrounded by cheerleader parents. The guys and I talked

strategy the whole game and I enjoyed their astute knowledge

of football.

Once again, I was stunned at the warmth and

friendliness of the fans we met. After the game I told Kevin

Henry we'd probably be back in two weeks for the Iron Bowl

when Auburn and Alabama would run head-on into each other.

Kevin said, "If you do, I'll give you two tickets and you can sit

with me." Wow! It's hard to imagine how wonderful people are until you get off your couch, out of your comfort zone, and go to a ballgame.

Kevin must've taken two hundred pictures with his fancy camera before halftime, and I thought he must be part Japanese with all the shutter-clicking. Then he tells me his daughter is an Auburn cheerleader. His oldest daughter, who graduated last year, was also a cheerleader, and his youngest daughter has been asked to be a cheerleader next year. I said, "Wow, snap away!" Kevin played baseball at Auburn with Vincent Bo Jackson, and his wife was on the gymnastic team. Great Tiger family.

Then, before we get to the game, this little note: ever wondered how Auburn's eagle is trained to fly around the stadium, but always land at midfield and not in the next county? During game week, they only feed the eagle each day when he lands at midfield. So he has to work to get fed. I'm familiar with that technique. Jenny uses it often.

The Game

Sometimes words can't begin to describe what it's like when you experience something that causes you to transcend normal emotions at a ballgame. Like, the Cubs or Red Sox winning the World Series after a hundred years of futility. Like, the New Orleans Saints winning the Super Bowl after decades of being the "Ain'ts" and I was on Bourbon Street the night the Saints won the Super Bowl and I can tell you firsthand about the outpouring of glee and unbridled joy that was indescribable.

Ever since my father took me to my first LSU game, I learned to watch the crowd after a big play when they were yelling the loudest, and to soak up the electricity. It's still sort of an adrenaline rush to just look around and realize you are in the middle of a tsunami of unrestrained happiness and fevered emotion.

Cheering for a home underdog in an important game with an intense fan base is the ultimate. You know getting pounded is a possibility, but as the game progresses and you realize beating the big bad Goliath is becoming more than a mere possibility, the tsunami begins to rise. It was happening in this game, and still Auburn fans were cautiously optimistic, because beating a No. 1 team is rare.

Georgia started the game by taking the opening series and quickly marching down for a TD. I looked at Jenny and said, "That was too easy. This might get ugly." But Auburn answered with a field goal, and slowly the momentum began to turn. Georgia's vaunted rushing attack was stuck in concrete. At the half, Auburn had forged a nine-point lead and the fans were beginning to believe.

In the second half, Georgia made numerous mistakes that led to more Auburn points and the rout was on. Georgia couldn't run, pass, tackle, or block and that's gonna get you taken to the woodshed. Auburn treated the 'Dogs like a rented mule caravan. As the time mercifully ticked off, the tsunami grew higher and higher. I thought maybe we might rush the field since we were on row six and next to the student section, but Kevin said in his fifty years the "Kick-Six" win over Bama

in 2013 was the only time he had ever seen the field rushed. So

here we were with that rarity of rarities happening right in front

of us. The underdog home team was winning a monumental

game with fans going crazy! Does it get any better than this?

Van Moates, a former player who rode on the shuttle with us,

said this was one of the five greatest wins in Auburn history

with the 17-16 game and the kick-six game two others.

FINAL SCORE: AUBURN 40, GEORGIA 17

WINNERS AND LOSERS

Winners

1) MIAMI: Now that Preacher Richt is in charge of the U,

you'd have to say this was Choirboys vs. Catholics. Only

problem is, the choirboys should go to confession after the

bully beat-down they laid on Notre Dame. They will move up

to No. 2 in the poll now, and may have returned to their former

glory. **MIAMI 41, NOTRE DAME 8**

2) AUBURN: After the LSU loss, the Auburn Tigers had serious questions about their team and its coach. This win was a statement, and Bama had better watch out. Lose to Auburn, and the Tigers go to the SEC Championship, and Bama might be out of the playoffs. The Iron Bowl will be a test of iron will, and iron strength, and if Auburn plays like they did against Georgia, Bama's steel nerves will be melted into little steel eagles for sale in Toomer's Drug Store.

3) CFP CHAOS: Seems like every week we have a new set of players. Bama has been the only constant, but that may change soon. This week's upsets opened the door for an additional six to eight teams' hopes to make the playoffs if things fall their way. This just may well be, for more reasons than one, the greatest fall of all.

Losers

1) GEORGIA: The Bulldogs got eaten alive by the Tiger-Eagle-Plainsmen things to put their playoff hopes in jeopardy.

Win-out the rest of the season and they may be back in, but for now, so much for the hype about being better than Bama.

2) NOTRE DAME: Although I called this game "Catholics vs. Choirboys," since they've been out of trouble lately and Preacher Richt is on the pulpit, "Convicts" may be more appropriate since Miami cuffed 'em, locked 'em up. and threw away the key.

3) ANYBODY NOT NAMED MAYFIELD: Barkley of Penn State, Adams of Notre Dame, J. T. Barrett of Ohio State, you guys might be invited to the ceremonies, but don't get too excited. Baker has studied his recipe, mixed the ingredients, cooked up the entree, and is ready to enjoy the dessert. Baker Mayfield will clinch the Heisman Trophy.

NEXT WEEK'S GAME: No. 22 MICHIGAN @ No. 5 WISCONSIN

I've heard about the beauty of Madison, Wisconsin, and Lake Mendota that the town was founded on. It'll be a treat to see it.

Plus, all the Big 10 fans I've met say Wisconsin fans are wild

and party like its 1999. Best of all, is the weather forecast for

Saturday has temperatures in the 30s and a 90 percent chance

of snowfall. Let it snow, let it snow, let it snow! Now this will

be REAL football! If Wisconsin wins they only need to win-

out the season and they will be in the playoffs. No one around

the country believes they are that good, and just last week I

trolled their schedule. So now it's time to put up or close your

pie hole. Did I tell you its gonna snow? I'm dreaming of a

white ballgame.

Well, Badger's won!

WEEK TWELVE: WISCONSIN VS. MICHIGAN
CAMP RANDALL STADIUM

MADISON, WISCONSIN

No. 19 Michigan @ No. 5 Wisconsin

Wolverines vs. Badgers

The Pleasant Peninsula State vs. The Land of Milk and Honey

The Wisconsin football team should adopt Rodney Dangerfield for their mascot. For those too young to know who Rodney Dangerfield was, he was a famous comedian in the '70s and early '80s who always started off his show saying, "I don't get

no respect." Most voters in the polls don't respect their

schedule, recruiting, stadium, or coach. They are always

ranked low in the recruiting polls every year, though they have

won more games than any big time university since 2014

except Clemson, Ohio State, and Alabama.

The key to their success was started by the godfather of

Wisconsin football, Barry Alvarez, who came to Madison in

1990, and coached through the end of the 2005 season. You

might say he built a fence around the state and kept all the

good instate players for the Badgers. Then he started a

meaningful walk-on program, and also developed two- and

three-star players into four-star players. When Barry Alvarez

was hired, at his press conference he boasted, "You'd better get

some season tickets now, 'cause in a few years there won't be

any." They still show that clip as part of the pregame show to

fire everyone up.

Alvarez's blueprint worked.

In 1993, his fourth year at Wisconsin, they won their

first Big 10 title in 30 years. During Alvarez's sixteen-year stay

at Wisconsin, his teams won three Rose Bowls, played in

eleven bowls, and he retired as the winningest coach in Badger

history. The success continues, and going into this game the

Badgers are 10-0 for the first time in history.

This team can only be described as a blue collar team,

with small town players from remote frozen places, and walk-

ons who are treated like scholarship players with the same gear

and lockers as the starters. Since 1990, nineteen walk-ons have

gone on to play in the NFL, including three-time NFL

defensive player of the year, J.J.Watts. And 47 of their 85

scholarship players are from rural Wisconsin towns. The

coaching staff's loyalty to the university runs just as deep.

Wisconsin is the only Top 25 team whose head coach and top

two coordinators are grads from the school where they coach.

Wisconsin has developed a solid winning program, and I

would caution against disrespecting this team. And remind

readers that Rodney Dangerfield laughed all the way to the

bank.

The Hype

Michigan is the all-time winningest program in big time

football. And even with the success of the Wisconsin team, still

the Badgers have been beaten by the Wolverines more times

than the Harlem Globetrotters beat their patsy rivals the

Washington Generals. In fifty of the sixty-five games they've

played, the Wisconsin Badgers were skinned and hung out to

dry. Because of the record, the Wisconsin fans are "cautiously

optimistic" to win this one.

Since Wolverines and Badgers are cousins, I wondered

if the fans had any animosity between them. I got my answer in

a hurry when an otherwise nice fan I talked to at the first

tailgate saw a Michigan fan, and immediately said, "Welcome

to Madison and f... you." The Michigan fan slowed, but

thought twice about it, and decided a finger gesture was

sufficient reply. During the game, a Wisconsin fan behind me yelled at the referees for penalties the entire game. And a Michigan fan also behind me said, "That guy wouldn't know a penalty if it slapped him in the face, which is what I'm about to do." Sooo, ok, we're talking fan intensity here on the level of Bama/Auburn, or Clemson/South Carolina, or Ohio State/ Michigan. At least the fans were friendly to me.

Wisconsin needs this win badly for street cred, and to convince the CFP committee they belong in the Top Four. And Mr. Khakipants, Michigan's coach Jim Harbaugh, also needs this win badly to restore his fans' trust in him.

The Sights

You don't need off-campus sights to visit when you have a campus as beautiful as the University of Wisconsin and its adjoining pristine Lake Mendota, with the water lapping up onto the campus lawn.

Founded in 1849, and presently home to 30,000

students, the university claims many outstanding scientific

discoveries. In 1911, two professors made discoveries that

paved the way for modern nutritional sciences, and continued

with further advancements that in 1913, and 1916, when

vitamin A and vitamin B were discovered by Elmer McCollom,

a university professor. In 1923, another professor discovered a

way to introduce Vitamin D into milk. And in 1988, University

of Wisconsin labs were first to isolate and culture human

embryonic stem cells.

Lake Mendota is known for its boating, and fishing,

and you can rent both fishing and sailing boats. There are

numerous fishing guides to show anglers just where to find

smallmouth bass.

Madison is the state capitol of Wisconsin, and the

capitol building is the tallest building in the city by state law.

Legislation prohibits buildings in town from being any higher

than the 187-foot columns on the capitol building. A visit is well worth the time, and so it the Henry Vilas Zoo, considered

one of the best zoos in America. It's the only one I know of

that charges no admission or parking fees. The Olbrich

Botanical gardens are beautiful and designed to be lovely in all

seasons, whether covered in snow or bathed in sunshine.

And then there's Camp Randal stadium, the oldest

stadium in the Big 10 Conference, and holds over 80,000 fans.

The Food and the Fans

I must apologize in advance to readers for the lack of personal

time spent this week on food and tailgating. Last week was my

busiest week at work this year, and I couldn't get here until late

Friday. Couple that with an 11 a.m. kickoff, and this week's

material may not be what you are use to. If this were a video

blog, maybe I could rely on my good looks and charm to

bedazzle you this week. But, since it's not...so, ok, I'll give you

what I've got.

Madison with 250,000 residents, has many great food options. For breakfast, go to Mickies Dairy Bar, billed as "a breakfast eatery with communal tables" and order whatever, but make sure to order only one pancake. It's one block from campus and a Badger tradition for decades, and their pancakes are as big as yo' mama.

As far as steakhouses are concerned, Smoky's Club is a local landmark, casual and decorated with local artifacts, along with Fleming's Prime Steakhouse, a high-end midwest chain like our Southern Ruth's Chris. Both these spots are the crowd favorites. Delaney's is also a white-tablecloth place for steaks and anything else. And, Lombardi's is the go-to Italian place.

Tailgating here is quite different from everywhere else. In fact, its not really tailgating, its pub-gating. There are thirty different pubs around the campus and most of the pregame eating and drinking is done along this trail of pubs. And "here" is where the gathering of Badger fans shine and really bring out their team spirit. Man, these people are hard core and can outdrink Dean Martin and Charlie Sheen combined. Maybe the

fact that many are also Green Bay Packers fans and come in

from the frozen tundra of Lambeau Field helps to explain the

energy in the pubs, which matches tailgating anywhere, just a

different venue for getting together. By now, all my readers

could guess that I'm partial to food and fun that goes on right

outside the stadium. As one of their songs goes, and sung to the

Budweiser tune, "When you say Wisconsin, you've said it all."

My favorite bars would have to be The Wise at the

Hotel Red, Lucky's, The Library—is there a school that doesn't

have a bar called the Library—and The Red Zone. Then, Dave

and Mary from New Berlin told me visitors have got to

experience the Jump Around, and the Fifth Quarter. And Fred,

a '56 grad, and his son Mark, both said the same. Hmmm, a

pattern seems to develop. The only Fifth Quarter I ever knew

involved heavy drinking during a tradition known as going to

the whip, that grew up during a time when LSU had eight

losing seasons in eleven years.

My usual protocol, where I find myself outside the stadium looking for a way in was not looking so good. Tickets, so far, have always been easy to come by, but after fifteen minutes the only ones I saw were in the hands of scalpers. They had a pair and weren't willing to sell just one.

I was debating what to do, when the strangest thing happened. This whole year I have felt like the last of a dying breed, not running into anyone who is doing what I'm doing, and what's more, neither have I even heard of anyone else who's attempted this odyssey. While holding up one finger, which of course means I'm looking for one ticket, making sure to hold up the correct finger, another man comes towards me also holding up one finger. He asked me if I had one ticket, and I thought this guy isn't very well versed in how this works. So I said, "No I *need* one ticket." He said, "I just passed a guy with two but won't separate them. You wanna buy 'em and sit together?" So I said, "Ok, I'm in."

Then as we walked towards the ticket dude, this guy

said, "I'm from Atlanta and I've been going to the biggest game

every week." Whoa! There's another one of me!? I said, "Say

that again, I think I misunderstood what you just said." He

looked at me with pride, smiling, and said, "I've gone to

different ballgames all over the country this year except for

three or four weekends. The first weekend I was at the UCLA/

Texas A&M game," he said.

Okay, that wasn't the highest ranked game and he

missed some weekends. Whew! Close call. My new friend is in

the minor league, but I was mighty glad to run into somebody

even close to my story. Steve from Johns Creek, Georgia was

knowledgeable and friendly, and we decided to maybe meet up

again at the Rose Bowl with Jenny, Eddie, and Meagan. With

Steve sitting next to me, I also met Tom Mollerleile, and his

son, Matt who sat in front of me. They said they pick one or

two games a year and leave the brutal cold of Minnesota to

experience college football where it's warmer. The best time

they ever had was at LSU, and it turned them into Tiger fans.

The concessions were, yep, you guessed it, we are back

in the Midwest...brats. They were better than Ohio State's, and

similar to Penn State's, but the best concessions were the

cheese curds. Now, there's a dish that needs a new name.

Cheese curds are the solid pieces of curdled milk, fried, and

eaten with a dip. Yeah, sounds nasty, but it tastes like

mozzarella sticks to me in a nugget form. I first had cheese

curds at the LSU/Wisconsin game at Lambeau Field last year,

and I can recommend them despite their name.

The Game

There is an indoor tailgate party at the old gymnasium with

live bands and concessions that was not only cool, but also

warm. Cool as in fun, and warm as in not cold. Outside it was

frigid, and the forecast was for snow. So, I was excited about

the possibility of a full game in the snow, and although it was snowing on the way to the game, it stopped when I got to the stadium.

The old gym where the indoor tailgate party was, is built right up against the stadium, and from inside the stadium at that end you can see the windows and relief of the building. Makes for an interesting backdrop with architectural character. Although the stadium holds 80,000, it seems a lot smaller than that. When I took my seat with my new best friends, Steve, Jack, and Lyle, I immediately realized this was the tightest seat I'd ever sat in, and there's not even a close second. Probably four inches narrower, and some five inches less legroom than seating in other stadiums. When I complained to Jack, a '56 grad, he said, "Well, it gets cold up here, and closer together you'll stay warmer. Go Badgers!"

I couldn't tell if everyone here is bigger, or if all the layered clothing made us turn sideways to fit into our seats. I had so many layers on I looked like Nanook of the North.

The band had the usual pregame show that was cool, as in a good show, and also as in thirty-three degrees, and wet, and the way they double- timed it across the field warmed up everyone's spirits, and we were ready for the battle about to begin.

At first, Badger fans and Wolverine fans alike sensed that Michigan was the better team. Their passing game was working well, and they took the lead in the second quarter. Wisconsin couldn't move the ball, and the home crowd got nervous. The only score for Wisconsin was on a fluke punt return for a TD. My NBF's said the Badgers are a second-half team, just wait. I didn't have the heart to tell them they needed new players, not a new half.

But when the second half began, the Badgers looked like a different team. All of a sudden they were moving the ball at will and Michigan's offense was looking like the French army with only reverse gears.

At the end of the third quarter it was time for "Jump

Around." When the House Of Pain's song of the same name

began to blare over the loudspeakers, the entire crowd began to

jump up and down and the press box and upper decks began to

sway. In fact, in 2003, university officials decided all that

jumping around might cause structural damage to the venerable

old stadium, and they cancelled "The Jump." Problem is, they

didn't tell the fans, and when the fourth quarter began without

"The Jump" the fans rained a firestorm on the sound guy and

administrators. The student section sat in protest, booed the

entire fourth quarter, and raised their middle fingers to the

press box chanting, "F... the sound guy!" Shocked

administrators held a meeting the next day after an avalanche

of protest, and got an engineer to say no damage would occur

from "The Jump," and it resumed the next game. POWER TO

THE PEOPLE!

By the time the game was over, it was apparent

Wisconsin was the better team, and Mr. Khaki Pants wasn't a

happy camper. Then came ,one of those events that you will see only in college football. Pay attention, 'cause this is really cool. The Wisconsin band raced back on the field and played a bunch of songs that everyone in the stadium could sing or dance to. Meanwhile, the band spread out in groups all over the field, doing crazy things. They played while lying down, played while break dancing on the field and running all over the place, danced with each other and the cheerleaders, and generally had a blast. The fans who stayed—a big crowd because of the big victory—were going crazy dancing and singing. THIS is something every university band should think about doing. The Fifth Quarter is what its called and it was extremely cool!

I started to leave before they were through, but I turned around and decided to stay and watch two more songs A voice in my head told me I might never be here again, so soak it up a little longer. The only band I've ever seen having this much fun is the Stanford Band, who are allowed to wear whatever they want and run around doing crazy things during halftime. All in, it was a crazy good time and a great win for the home team. I hope I can come back so I can give Madison and the University of Wisconsin a longer and better visit.

FINAL SCORE: WISCONSIN 23, MICHIGAN 10

<u>WINNERS AND LOSERS</u>

Winners

1) Wisconsin: Keep disrespecting the Badgers at your own risk. I'm guilty of trolling their schedule on more than one occasion, but they answered the bell and showed they could beat Ohio State in the conference championship and go to the playoffs. Michigan got hit in the mouth in the second half and looked like a Roberto Duran beat-down while screaming "No mas, no mas!"

2) Lamar Jackson: Louisville's QB, last year's Heisman winner, has had an equally outstanding year-after. But there's

less hype for a previous winner, and voters aren't inclined to vote for a repeat winner. Because of that, and the fact his team isn't doing as well as last year, he will be invited to the ceremonies but won't win. Despite this, he hasn't said a word in defiance and just keeps doing his job.

3) Justin Motlow: It's not very often we talk about a walk-on player, but Justin, a seldom used wide receiver for Florida State, snatched his first career touchdown late in Florida State Seminoles' 77-6 win over Delaware State, becoming the first member of the Seminole tribe to actually score for the Seminoles.

Losers

1) Season ticket holders at many Power Five Universities: REALLY?! Bama/Mercer?, Auburn/ULM? Clemson/Citadel? Come on guys, let's give back to the people who support you and give them a game that doesn't resemble the Tyson/Botha fight in January, 1999. Botha pretended to fight for five rounds and finally lowered his gloves and said, "Hit me!" Tyson

proceeded to do just that and knocked him out. I guess boxing isn't the only sport that can take a fall for a paycheck.

2) Baker Mayfield: Yes, I know. He's going to win the Heisman, but, you don't have to do it in Trump fashion. Not being political here, it's just a fact that Trump is, shall I say, emotional to the extreme sometimes. And when Oklahoma had smoked Kansas, Mayfield, near the end of the game, began screaming profanity at the Kansas sideline and grabbing his crotch. The award is supposed to exemplify sportsmanship, also, so maybe his belated apology will suffice.

3) Nebraska: Things have gotten so bad the Cornhuskers gave up 50 points in consecutive games for the first time since 1945. Cornhusker is appropriate, since the team has been shucked and eaten. This team is softer than creamed corn. Yes, I can get cornier if they don't shape up. Scott Frost at Central Florida, a Nebraska native, will maybe get on a plane to Lincoln and help out, as soon as he finishes the successful season he's having at Central Florida.

PENN STATE 56, NEBRASKA 44

NEXT WEEK'S GAME: No. 1 ALABAMA @ No. 9

AUBURN

This is going to be a classic Iron Bowl. Alabama is an early 4-point favorite, which surprises me since Auburn looked so good against Georgia, and the game's in Auburn. There have been many classics in this series, but Alabama has dominated overall, winning 45 of 81 games. I have heard from many fans that their rivalry with so-and-so university is the biggest rivalry. Forget it. This is THE most intense, passionate, and over-the-top rivalry in college football. When you're born in Alabama, you are told by your parents who you'll pull for, and you'd better do it or you'll be excommunicated from the family. If you move into the state, the first question you're asked is, "Are you gonna support the Tigers, or that other school?" My Tide, or West Georgia? This Iron Bowl will be loud, intense, and there will be serious repercussions for the losing fans. So everybody have a great Thanksgiving, and then come back ready for the last regular season weekend of the

year. I'm tired, yes, but this season coming to an end soon is

kinda sad.

Rolling Toomer's Corner (The closest to a snow game that I have been to)

WEEK 13: AUBURN VS. ALABAMA

JORDAN-HARE STADIUM

AUBURN, ALABAMA

The Hype

The Tide vs. The Tigers

Pachyderms vs. Plainsmen

Ever since the first college football game in 1869 between

Princeton and Rutgers, fans and players alike have argued over

which rivalry is the most intense. In the minds of Ohio State and Michigan fans, their rivalry is more intense than Uma

Thurman in *Kill Bill*. In the hearts of Clemson and South

Carolina fans their rivalry is more vicious than a pit bull fight.

Guess a cock fight would have been more appropriate, but at

least I laid off Michael Vick this time. In the souls of every

Georgia and Georgia Tech fan they will tell you that "Clean

Old Hate" is a docile term for their rivalry.

And there are many more rivalries around the country

where fans, coaches and players wait all year for The Big One.

The rivalry game is known to push fans beyond the normal

bounds of decency and decorum. People turn into screaming,

panting, and foaming-at-the-mouth idiots. But, its just a sport.

Right? Wrong! A college football rivalry is fought for peace,

for tranquility, and for the other inalienable rights under the

constitution such as freedom from being ragged for a year and

the right to boast without limits. And this Alabama/Auburn

Iron Bowl rivalry supersedes all others. Fans' emotions can

flow like molten lava, as when one such eruption killed the

Toomer's Oaks, as we wrote about earlier.

The Iron Bowl between Alabama and Auburn has been

fought since 1893, and is so named because of Birmingham's

historic role in the steel industry when the game was played in

Birmingham every year at Legion Field. Auburn's famous

coach "Shug" Jordan once said, "We don't need a bowl game,

we play in the iron bowl every year." Auburn was the first to

bring its home game of the Iron Bowl to Jordan-Hare Stadium

beginning in 1991, then Alabama followed suit in 2000 when

they moved their home game with Auburn to Bryant-Denny

Stadium.

When I first began researching this rivalry, I had no

idea it extended so deeply into the culture, history and

founding of the schools. The University of Alabama was

established in 1831, and Auburn University in 1856, under the

name East Alabama Male College. Bama tried for the next

seventy years to either close Auburn or absorb it. The fights in the state legislature were vicious with Bama legislators

attempting to defund Auburn for decades. As one Alabama

administrator put it, "Auburn is an illegitimate child...born out

of the misery of the Reconstruction Period."

Man, this stuff goes REAL deep! When I lived in

Mississippi and Louisiana, I was aware, of course, of the

football rivalry between Bama and Auburn, but now that I

make my home in Alabama, I can tell you this rivalry is woven

passionately into the very fabric of all walks of life and

demographics of the entire state.

There have been many classic games in this series, and

because of the consistently successful football programs of

Bama and Auburn over the years, this game has become more

meaningful than any other SEC rivalry. Over the last sixty

years, one of these two teams has won the conference

championship in thirty-three of those years. And this

weekend's game is only the second winner-take-all for the SEC

West division. The first was in 2013, when Auburn won by

returning a missed field goal for a touchdown on the last play,

known as the "Kick Six" game.

Ryan Fowler, a radio host on a sports station in

Tuscaloosa says, "If this game lives up to its hype, it could be

the most important in Iron Bowl in history. Nick Saban has a

chance to beat Auburn for a fourth consecutive time, and that

hasn't happened since Bear Bryant in 1983.

Prior to 2009, in many of the previous big Iron Bowls,

the winning team didn't have a clear path to the National

Championship. But, since 2009, the winner of the Iron Bowl

has gone on many times to play for the National Championship

either by the BCS, or the new four-team playoff system. And

then in this game, there's the matter of rumors swirling around

about Auburn's coach Gus Malzahn possibly leaving to go

home to coach the University of Arkansas, who just fired their

coach. So, let's tee it up, and kick it off, and let the fun begin!

Sights and Food

Normally we separate these two sections, but, because of a shortage of time this weekend we combined them.

Although most of the sights and food options in the Auburn/Opelika area were mentioned in our Week Eleven game, readers told us about other places to consider. The Hound is the top rated breakfast spot, but many Auburn fans told us their favorite breakfast place was Crepe Myrtle Cafe, or Big Blue Bagel.

The Hound's brunch where we ate, includes their Redneck Benedict which is scratch biscuits, with house bacon, scrambled eggs, and sausage gravy. The Shrimp & Grits is covered with a delicious andouille cream sauce and the Silver Dollar Pancakes are cooked to perfection.

Our dinner at the Acre was mouthwatering, with their signature dishes being the beef short ribs, and the "Butt-Rubbed" Swordfish. For dessert, I had the Sweet Corn Pudding covered with a raspberry glaze and topped with vanilla ice

cream.

Niffer's Place is another Auburn tradition that needs to

be mentioned. With the best wings in town, they are also

known for their burgers, fries, and "fishbowl" drinks served in

a lively atmosphere. As far as sights I didn't mention before, I

was told Jule Collins Smith Museum of Fine Art is a small but

interesting place, and a visit well worth your time.

Golfers are drawn to the area because of the number of

fine courses, including the crown jewel Robert Trent Jones

Grand National course. Mr. Jones said before he built the

course it was the single greatest site he had ever seen. It is the

host of the PGA's Barbasol Championship in July and boast 54

holes of magnificent golfing.

The Fans

Well, kinda disappointing this trip due to the unbelievable

traffic jam we encountered. We caught a shuttle off-campus for the ride in, just like we did for the Georgia game, but this time

it took almost three hours to get to the stadium. Last time, it

took us thirty minutes. By the time we finally got to the

stadium, it was time to find our Auburn benefactor, Kevin

Henry, whom we spoke of two weeks ago and get into the

stadium. As we were waiting for Mike and Kim, who are

friends of Kevin, to bring us our tickets, we somehow wound

up in front of the band in the street next to the stadium. Two

couples also standing nearby caught sight of us and one of the

men asked if I was Ed, the blogger. Guess I've developed a

new last name. I said, "Yes, how'd you know?" Cause Kevin

Henry told us about you, they offered, and your LSU

sweatshirt gave you away. They wanted to follow the blog, and

I handed out about the 3,000th card so far this year. They were

cheerleader parents, like Kevin and his wife, and asked did I

wear the same clothes I wore for the Georgia game. They

agreed that an LSU fan pulling for them would surely bring

good luck. "Yep," I said, "right down to the socks and

underwear, washed of course."

The Game

It's rare when a game of this magnitude lives up to it's hype,

but this one did that and more. Immediately upon entering the

stadium, anybody could tell this was no ordinary college

football game.

The stadium was full forty-five minutes before kickoff,

and the looks on the fans faces told you all you needed to

know. Auburn fans were cautiously optimistic and smiling but

not laughing. Bama fans were laughing and ignoring Auburn

fans who said "War Eagle." Most Bama fans seemed to

believed they would win convincingly, confidence born out of

a continually winning track record that would make anybody

feel invincible. However, this is college football. Eighteen to

twenty-two-year old men cannot always play like you want

them to. The pendulum of performance must swing. So you can't take anything for granted. You only know when it's over.

When the pregame fly-over roared above the crowd, all went wild, and I waited for the eagle flyover. But something went wrong. The eagle flew majestically for a minute, then dive-bombed the fans in the end zone, and got so confused he landed not at midfield, but in the end zone. I looked at Kevin Henry's daughter, Sommer, a graduated Auburn cheerleader, and her friends and asked if that had ever happened before. She said, "Once, a long time ago, the eagle flew out of the stadium." I figured this was a bad sign. The tidal wave of emotion began washing wave after wave the entire game. This was surely going to be the loudest and most exciting game of the year.

On GameDay, Charles Barkley, a former Auburn basketball player, was the guest picker and when it came time to pick the winner of this game, he was the only person who picked Auburn. He said, "You remember the Kick-Six game?

Well, this is going to be the Kick-Ass game." And boy was he right! Auburn dominated the trenches and ran and threw the ball well on offense during the entire game. Alabama made some mistakes they don't usually make, but that was because of the pressure Auburn applied.

Now, two weeks in a row Auburn has defeated the No. 1 team. Beat Georgia in the rematch this Saturday for the SEC Championship, and they will be in the four-team playoff. Bama has been showing chinks in their armor for a few weeks now, and no one should be surprised at the outcome. Disappointed, yes, because Auburn just flat out beat 'em! At the end of the game, as the fans rushed the field for only the second time in Auburn history, I thought why not!? So I went down and melted into the thousands of fans, students, and players and enjoyed a fitting high-energy conclusion to the regular season of The Greatest Fall Of All.

After the game, I met a nice couple on the shuttle who lives in Kennesaw, Georgia. Chad and Jennifer Ward, Auburn fans, want to meet us next week. They also said they wanted us to host them for an LSU game next year. I think that makes about a hundred people now. Gonna be a hell of a tailgate. Chad said his uncle, a Mr. Sprinkle played for Bear Bryant, was responsible for doing away with the Bear. I said, "What? Didn't he die of a heart attack?" Chad answered, "Yes, but my uncle was a pall bearer." Ok, got me on that one.

I've said a number of times how I wanted to go to a snow game, and if you could see a pic of Toomer's Corner after the game, you'd see the closest I've come so far.

FINAL SCORE AUBURN 26, ALABAMA 14

WINNERS AND LOSERS

Winners

1) Auburn and College Football: By beating Alabama, Auburn not only did something good for themselves, they also showed

everyone that the 900-pound gorilla that is Saban's Alabama is beatable. The win also opened the door for many other teams to dream about playing for, and winning, a National Championship. This team is exciting and represents what all of us can identify with when we take on adversity and use it as incentive to reach our lofty goals.

2) Clemson: Now the reigning National Champs find themselves in familiar territory, No. 1 in the country again! If Bama somehow gets in the playoff, the first semi-final will probably be a rematch of last years Championship.

CLEMSON 34, SOUTH CAROLINA 10

3) Quinton Flowers: South Florida's QB had 605 yards of offense by himself! His five touchdowns could earn him the player of the week, and his season totals and performances should have him in the Heisman discussion.

Losers

1) Tennessee: Just when you thought the Vols had sunk as low as the Marianna Trench, they create yet another bad milestone.

Before this weekend, Ohio State and Tennessee were the only two big boy football teams that had never had an eight-game losing season in their entire HISTORY. But after being sunk by the Vanderbilt Commodores, Tennessee's ship made like the Titanic, and broke in half and sunk to an eight-loss season. Now only Ohio State can say they've never in their history had an eight-loss season or worse. **VANDERBILT 42, TENNESSEE 24**

2) Jim Harbaugh, Michigan's coach: Mr. Khaki Pants curious adventure at Michigan is beginning to smell like green eggs and ham. Maybe if he didn't sleep in those khaki pants, he would wake up from Goodnight Moon with a better game plan than Big Bird Right, Big Bird Left, and Big Bird Fly. If things don't get better next year, he's gonna lose his Wonka golden ticket and become the Cat In The Hat. **OHIO STATE 31, MICHIGAN 20**

3) The Pac 12 Conference: Hey, Left Coast, you're OUT! You have good teams, but no great ones. You're always talking

about your QBs and how much more exciting you are. But

bottom line is, year in and year out, your teams can't compete

with the SEC, ACC or Big 10 conferences. Recruit better, and

coach better, or you're gonna become as hard to find as the

dodo bird.

NEXT WEEK'S GAME: AUBURN vs. GEORGIA, FOR

THE SEC CHAMPIONSHIP

We thought the biggest game was going to be the ACC

Championship, but when Miami lost to Pitt Friday, the SEC

game became the highest ranked. This is a replay of Week 11 at

Auburn, and if you'll look back at that game, you will learn

more about the oldest rivalry in the South. Auburn won handily

the first time, but they'd better bring their A-game, 'cause I've

been to this rodeo before! When LSU lost to Alabama in the

2011 National Championship, it was a rematch of the regular

season game where LSU won in Tuscaloosa. In fact, sports

writers and commentators said LSU had the greatest regular

season in history. But alas, as the fourth quarter dwindled down

to a 21-0 Bama win, I realized how hard it is to beat a quality

team twice in the same season. Offering proof of this, after the

game I read that the same scenario had happened twenty times

before in big bowl games, and the winner in fifteen of those

rematches lost in the first game. Be careful Auburn, rematches

are tough. Regardless of the outcome, it will be a fantastic

game, with the winner headed to the College Football Playoffs!

Mercedes Benz Stadium: SEC Championship Game

WEEK FOURTEEN: THE SEC CHAMPIONSHIP, GEORGIA VS. AUBURN

MERCEDES-BENZ STADIUM

ATLANTA, GEORGIA

The Hype

Since expanding in 1992, the SEC has held a conference

championship game after the regular season between the

winners of the East and West divisions. Although the Auburn/

Georgia game is the oldest rivalry in the South, this is the first time they've played for the championship since the conference

became two divisions.

In Week 11, these teams played at Auburn with the

Tigers taking the Bulldogs to the pound and locking them up.

Unfortunately for Auburn, the Dogs were not euthanized at the

pound and won the right for redemption by winning the East

Division of the SEC and the right to play them again. When I

was in law school, we learned an axiom of law that still holds

true today, "Every dog is allowed one bite." At the first

meeting, these Dogs were toothless, but my how revenge and

three weeks can grow some teeth in the jaws of a mad junkyard

dog. As I said in last week's game, I've seen this repeat rodeo

before, as have you, and we both know how it usually turns

out. I saw my LSU Tigers lose a repeat game in 1960 against

Ole Miss in the Sugar Bowl, and against Alabama in 2011 for

the National Championship, also in the Sugar Bowl.

Psychologically, it seems eighteen to twenty-two-year

olds think that just because they pound a team the first time, all they have to do is show up to win also a second round. The

loser of the first game, however, is angrier than a one-legged

man in a butt-kicking contest, and usually proceeds to try in a

rematch to drop-kick the other team into the next county. But,

this game is about more than revenge for little Kirby Smart,

Georgia's coach. The winner of this game gets into the four-

team playoff for the National Championship. And Georgia

hasn't won a National Championship since Herschel Walker

was running over people in 1980, and Marla Maples was a

freshman at Georgia. We will get to her later.

Georgia fans will certainly be very nervous about this

rematch, since their history for the last many years with the

previous coach was to climb the mountain, but never reach the

top.

Tickets are selling on the secondary market at the

highest price for any game we've gone to this year. Five

hundred will get you a nosebleed and a hotdog. The new

Mercedes-Benz Stadium in Atlanta only holds seventy-six

thousand and change, so that makes tickets even harder to get.

This is not going to be a skirmish, this will be a full-fledged

war of attrition and destruction.

The Food and the Sights

Due to time shortage we didn't have the usual time to spend on

sights and food so we put these sections together again.

Naming the best restaurants in Atlanta is like trying to pick out

the best Dallas Cowboy cheerleader. You can't go wrong.

Whether it's Bones or Chops for steaks, Soto Soto, Davio's, or

Bocca Lupo for Italian, or Chops Lobster Bar, or Atlanta

Seafood Market for seafood, the options are a lot more than in

Stillwater or Tuscaloosa. This is a big, big town.

The Varsity, serving their famous hot dogs and fries,

covers two city blocks. Iconic in the culture of Atlanta, it's

most famous employees were Erby Walker, and comedian

Nipsy Russell. Erby worked there for fifty-five years and his famous saying was, "Have your money out, and your food on

your mind, and I'll get you to the game on time." Nipsy started

his celebrity career by singing the Varsity menu and telling

jokes while car hopping.

We ate at Legal Seafood, and I can recommend the

lump crab dip, buffalo shrimp, fresh oysters, and fish and

chips. After the game, we ate at Dantanna's, which is only one

block from the stadium and was packed with party animals

celebrating or consoling themselves with plenty of adult

beverages. Sorry to say, Atlanta, but the concessions at the

stadium need lots of improvement. The hot dogs were burnt,

the drink machines were out of ice by the second quarter,

vendors were out of most condiments at the half, and no one

knew where The Varsity stand was. I was told it was on the

third floor, and after searching and asking again, was told the

second floor. After striking out, I was then told I'd find the

Varsity on the first floor, definitely! But no such luck. I gave up finally. You need to tighten up, Atlanta, and get your

concessions for the fans on a par with your great new stadium.

In Week One, Eddie and I went to the College Football

Hall of Fame and it was a great visit. Very creative, interactive

and informative whether you are a football fan or not you need

to visit. The Georgia Aquarium is rated by many as the best

aquarium in America. Not only is it huge, and contains as

many as 120,000 fish and sea creatures, it is also the only

aquarium that has a whale shark.

The CNN studio tour is interesting and quite

informative, and is located in the downtown area close to most

sights you'd want to see. Be sure to wear your MAKE

AMERICA GREAT AGAIN hat and you will probably be

escorted out of the building. The Fox Theater, also downtown,

was originally built as a lavish movie theater, but has since

become a venue for the cultural hub of Atlanta, hosting

Broadway shows, musicals, ballet performances, and concerts.

The Fans

The morning of the game, we bumped into Rick Catlett, president of the Gator Bowl. Rick, a Jacksonville resident and Florida fan, said he felt recently hired Dan Mullen would bring the Gators back to prominence. Rick said he personally knows Mullen, and is certain Florida will soon be back in the championship game.

When we were having lunch at Legal Seafood, we ate at the bar as usual. As I've opined before, that's where you meet the most interesting people. Once again, we were not disappointed. Right before we got our appetizers, a mid 50s gentleman sat next to us and asked, "Mind if an old dawg sits here?" I said, "Sure, if you don't mind sitting next to an old tiger." We got to talking about our odyssey, when I noticed his ring. I asked, and he said, "I played for Georgia when they won the 1980 National Championship." I asked what position. "Downfield blocker," he responded. Ok, there's no such thing, so where's he going with this, I wondered. "Herschel Walker was our running back, so mainly my job was to run downfield

and block. 'cause he was probably coming past the line of

scrimmage."

He told me his coach, Vince Dooley, wasn't well-liked

by most players, but they respected his ability to coach. When I

asked him about any interesting stories he had, he said his best

was off the field. When he was a senior in 1981, he began to

date a certain freshman named Marla Maples. Our new friend,

Lon Buckler, was Marla's boyfriend for the year until she

decided Georgia wasn't big enough for her, and she went to

New York to become a model. Later, after their breakup, both

went on to win the lottery. Lon won a Georgia lottery,

according to a friend of his I talked to, and Marla won the

Trump lottery. She pulled an end around on Trump's first wife,

Ivana, and scored a TD (Trump Down), causing a contentious

divorce and Donald's subsequent marriage to Marla. As Lon

said, "In college, she was eighteen going on twenty-four. She had five-star talent, a winning strategy, and the ability to

execute her game plan.

After the game, we ran into pretty boy "Loquacious"

Lon in Dantanna's, holding court in the lobby with his buddies,

and when last seen he was apparently still looking for the next

Marla Maples. When the game started, we were surrounded by

Georgia fans who seemed wound tighter than Spandex on a

sumo wrestler. They screamed at every single play, claiming

the referees were rigging the game because the SEC office

wanted Auburn to win. I'm not talking about one or two fans,

I'm talking about EVERY fan within twenty feet. They looked

normal enough, but they were foaming at the mouth over every

play screaming, "That was holding!" or, "That wasn't a

penalty!" Whatever they could come up with to blame the

referees for their slow start. Jenny and I said to each other we

hadn't experienced one fan this year who was that whiny on

every play.

After Georgia began to take control, I went and got

myself a Georgia hat and began to argue with them. "Hey, I'm

pulling for Georgia, but that wasn't a penalty." I finally noticed

that one guy had a white washcloth hanging out his pocket. I

asked him, "Why don't you pull out your crying towel and pass

it around?" I became a fan favorite, however, when they

noticed I had changed from an Auburn visor to a Georgia ball

cap.

As Georgia began to pull away, the formerly

hypercritical fans began to point to my hat and chant, "Fear the

hat, fear the hat." When it was over, everyone hugged, laughed,

and told Jenny and me they'd see us in Pasadena, with

promises of a lunch date.

The Game

Auburn struck first blood and went up 7-0. After kicking off,

they held the Dawgs and moved into scoring territory again.

With the best place kicker in football, Auburn was sure to go up at least 10-0. But then the wheels began to come off. They fumbled, and following that play and for the rest of the game, Georgia carried out an assault that would not end until all playoff hopes for Auburn's War Eagle was smothered.

By the third quarter, the locomotive that had been the Auburn offense pulled into Malfunction Junction. Plain and simple, Georgia wanted it more. They were better prepared and more motivated. The final score was indicative of the battle fought, and with the win Georgia moves on. I could go into more detail of certain momentum shifts and big plays but what's the point? When you lose by three TDs, you can't point to a couple plays or referee calls that made a big difference. Bottom line is you just got your booty whipped and your your War Eagle de-feathered. Thirty-seven years Georgia fans waited for this, and now maybe they have also won the confidence and stamina to reach the top of that mountain.

WINNERS AND LOSERS

Winners

1) Clemson: I never thought they'd be this good again in the consecutive season. Now the reigning National Champs are the No. 1 seed, and will play Bama in Clemson/Bama III. Their coach, Dabo Sweeny, is cornier than popcorn, and sometimes described as a "hayseed." But his players love him, and I'm not gonna argue with his sincerity and results. If you take him for granted, and think you're going to outsmart him, you'll find yourself in second place every time. **ACC CHAMPIONSHIP GAME: CLEMSON 38, MIAMI 13**

2) University of Central Florida: 13-0: For a University that I would say is new to the modern era of football, they are making serious waves in a state where Miami, Florida State, and Florida have dominated football for over a hundred years. Undefeated but unloved, this team and this university have an opportunity going forward to join big time football if the university makes the financial commitment necessary to this team. With the largest student body in the United States, as the years go on their alumni base will become huge soon and only

add to fan support. No team in the modern era has gone from being winless to undefeated in just two seasons.

3) New Mexico State: Why you ask? Because sometimes the smaller guys are deserving of recognition when they earn it. By beating South Alabama, the Aggies will go to a bowl for the first time in fifty-seven—that's five-seven-years. I'm guessing they might not even have a fan who's been to a bowl game?

Losers

1) Wisconsin: Rodney Dangerfield strikes again. "No respect, I don't get no respect." Well, you should have won, and then Ohio State fans wouldn't be cramming the psychologist's offices this week. Of course, they only have themselves to blame for losing by 31 to Iowa. The Buckeye fans are so livid over the playoff snub they've lost their vertical hold and have become nuttier than the Planters nut factory.

BIG 10 CHAMPIONSHIP GAME: OHIO STATE 27, WISCONSIN 21

2) Ohio State: Never mind, I think we covered that. How about, Florida Gators!? They didn't even play, but with Florida State's victory over the University of Louisiana-Monroe, the Gators became the only major college team in Florida that didn't qualify for a bowl. Guess we will have to start calling the Gators the "Laters."

3) Miami: Yes, I know, they only lost two games, and their future is brighter than the neon lights on South Beach. But if Pittsburgh in their previous game took them to the woodshed for a whipping, then Clemson took 'em to a dungeon and tortured them. Torture is what I'd call having to watch that 38-3 game. Maybe "Fifty Shades of Black and Blue" would be a good name for that film. And I've never understood why a coach goes for 3 when you are five touchdowns behind. Does he think getting off the goose egg means something? COME ON, MAN! Take a testosterone shot and go for a TD.

NEXT WEEK'S GAME: ARMY VS. NAVY

This should be a bucket list event whether you care about

football or not. This game epitomizes not only what's great

about our game, but also what's great about our country. The

color, pageantry, and passion between the cadets of Army and

Navy is pure and untainted by the pull of going on to

professional football. These players play for the pure

enjoyment of the game, and their loyalty to their chosen branch

of military service. Rare is the player in this game who will go

on to a pro contract. These two teams suit-up and play football

the way it used to be played in days gone by when amateurism

still produced five-star players, and the pure joy of being on

that field was all you needed to play your best. Jenny and my

brother from another mother, Glenn Roper, along with Luis

Rodriguez, our TCU host from Week Six, will enjoy every

wonderful moment in the snow that's forecast. This may be my

last chance at a snow game this season, so let's see what the

Army's The Long Gray Line, and the Navy Midshipmen will

do.

"Stormed the field"

WEEK FIFTEEN: ARMY VS. NAVY

LINCOLN FINANCIAL FIELD

PHILADELPHIA, PENNSYLVAINIA

The Hype

Army vs. Navy, 'nuff said!

Big Ed and Poppa both always said this is one of college

football's biggest games every year. I never understood why a

game between two unranked teams could garner so much

304 | *Ed Tonore*

interest and attention. And, since I've never been to this

historic game, researching and interviewing was imperative.

After digging and talking for days I began to realize

how different and special this rivalry is. When we talk about

college football rivalries, as we have throughout the book,

Auburn and Alabama, Michigan and Ohio State, South

Carolina and Clemson, Ole Miss and Mississippi State, are just

some of the many others that come to mind. And, one thing I

can tell you from first-hand experience, is many of those teams

and their fans do not respect the other teams and fans.

Occasionally you will find fans who are close friends with the

other side but usually the dislike of the other side far exceeds

the respect.

In this rivalry, commonly known as the Greatest

Rivalry in Sports, respect commands the day. In a game also

referred to as "America's Game," these teams and fans have a

respect for each other that exists due to a common calling.

Except for this day, they are on the same team, America's

military, with the purpose of defending and protecting our country. When talking to John Avard, from South Georgia, and his son Patrick, from Atlanta, John explained this interesting rivalry in a way we can all understand. John, a '67 West Point grad, was shot in the Vietnam war and if it wasn't for a Navy pilot dodging bullets while rescuing him and bringing him back to a hospital, he would have died.

But, on this day the men of the Army and the men of the Navy suit-up and battle each other like there's no tomorrow. There will be no professional contract waiting for these players, but winning this game is their team's mission and purpose. They will remember this game for the rest of their lives, and replay it over and over with glee or heartache. Shawn Flynn, an attorney in Boston and '95 grad of West Point, said he literally sobbed in the stands after last year's win for Army, which broke a 14-game losing streak to Navy. He said he looked around and saw dozens of grown men with tears in their eyes. When I asked Shawn how Navy was able to sustain such a winning streak, he said most people believe two things happened at the same time to tip the scales in Navy's favor. One, after 9/11 there were fewer high school grads enlisting in the Army because many felt that a long ground war was imminent, and being on a ship would be better than going house-to-house in Fallujah. The Navy had more athletic talent to choose from.

Second, to put it simply, Navy's coaching was better. Now, however, Army has turned a corner and their coach is very highly thought of as a man capable of leading them to victory. Also, enlistments are up as more people realize that the Army is not just about boots on the ground, but offers a host of job opportunities in various areas.

It should also be noted that The Commander-in-Chief's Trophy is at stake in this game. This trophy is only awarded in a year when either Army, Navy, or the Air Force Academy beats the other two teams. This year, both Army and Navy have beaten the Air Force, so the winner will get the prestigious

trophy.

As a fan bonus to me, as if the game and its pageantry and traditions weren't enough, snow is once again in the forecast for my game! Maybe this time this Tiger gets a snow day. Army vs. Navy, what a fitting high energy, rock'em-sock'em conclusion to the Greatest Fall of All. Yes, I'm going to the semi-final and championship games, but, technically, they will be played in the winter, not the fall.

This week we are accompanied by my best bud, Glenn Roper from Slidell, Louisiana. He said at the "internationally known" pre-season football party we have at home in Fairhope every year, that this would be the game he wanted to attend. So welcome to Philly, brother!

The Sights

The birthplace of freedom and democracy is, of course, in The City Of Brotherly Love, Philadelphia, Pennsylvania, and there is no shortage of iconic places to visit. We went to see the Liberty Bell, which is a must-see, and then stopped at the National Constitution Center for a live performance in a round theater of "We The People." It explores the founding of the country and tenets of the U.S. Constitution. Independence Hall, the birthplace of the Declaration of Independence and the Constitution, is required, but make sure you get a ticket first because sometimes they run out of time slots for walk-in visits. The last time I was there, it was around the anniversary of the first reading of the Declaration to a gathered crowd, and actors in period dress reenacted the reading. Very cool!

The United States Mint should be called the U.S. Walkathon because of the very long trek down a very long corridor, while looking down at the machines making coins, before turning around and hiking back the other way another half-mile while looking down at another hundred giant machines making coins. Honestly, not very exciting.

The Benjamin Franklin Museum, however, was interesting and very interactive. Ol' Ben was a heck of an inventor. We all learned in school about his kite, the lightning and electricity, his bifocals, the lightning rod, and the Franklin Stove. But, in the museum, I also discovered other interesting inventions he made. One, the glass armonica, incorporates wetting your finger and rubbing it on a glass to create sound. This instrument was about three feet long, and fitted with various widths of round glass for rubbing, and was a creative invention of Ben's. The music from it was said to sound like angels' voices.

You could probably spend a week seeing all the sights in Philly, so just go to the visitors' center in the Historic District and friendly, knowledgeable assistants will help you map out what to see. Lots of sports teams call Philadelphia home, and, interestingly enough the four professional teams each built their venues right next to each other. The Eagles football stadium, the Phillies baseball stadium, the NBA 76ers, and the NHL Flyers arenas are all bunched together. The

Phillies, by the way, are the oldest continuous team franchise

with one name in one city in all of pro American sports, dating

back to 1883.

The Food

Philadelphia is a veritable melting pot of ethnic groups and,

therefore, offers a smorgasbord of restaurants. Whether your

taste buds crave Italian or Vietnamese, American or Japanese,

or any other country's food, you can find it in Philly.

For lunch on Friday, we figured we had to try the one

thing everyone thinks of when it comes to Philly food, a Philly

cheesesteak. We went to Campo's and were told to be ready to

order 'cause if you don't know exactly what you want, you can

be ordered back to the end of the line. Talk about pressure! You

have to pick your bread, meat, type of cheese, what you want

on it, and how many, and be ready to order, or else. The

cheesesteaks were superb, and the owner who was very

friendly wanted to know if we liked 'em. Guess it showed that

we were newbies.

Our hosts for the Penn State/Michigan game from

weeks ago, Bill and Kim Kohl, took a train from Harrisburg to

meet us, and made reservations for us at Osteria, an Italian

restaurant with great reviews. Kenny Rapp, an attorney who

also hosted us at Penn State, was in town and met us as well,

and we all had drinks at a sister restaurant around the corner

before going to Osteria.

This meal was more like a gastronomical experience.

Where do I begin?! Bill and Kim's son, Christopher, is the

assistant manager, and I asked him what to order. Before he

could answer, I said, "Better yet, just feed me." Everyone at the

table agreed. What followed was the meal of a lifetime. I will

just list a few dishes from the sixteen-course meal we had,

along with a wine selection that would be the envy of

Wolfgang Puck. Five antipasti dishes started our king's feast,

and was followed by wild boar pasta, unbelievable ravioli so good we ordered three more dishes of the ravioli, and pork

belly scallop pasta. This all was followed by a delicious pan

roasted salmon, glazed rabbit over butter polenta, and whole

roasted and glazed duck.

Just when I thought I was so full I couldn't eat

anymore, our waiter told us dessert was on the way. Out comes

mousse and candied hazelnuts, fig and huckleberry crostata,

chocolate almond gelato, and malted almond milk. WOW!

Maybe the best meal I've ever had, and I've had some great

ones. Thanks again for everything Bill, Kim and Kenny. "We

Are...Penn State!" And I know they are reading this and

yelling back the same battle cry.

Concessions were maybe the best this year. Pulled pork

or chicken sandwiches, Philly cheesesteaks being cooked in

front of you with the air full of grilled steak aroma, a food

court with many selections, and the best hamburger I can

remember eating at a stadium. Ever. It had a fried egg on top,

and was covered in caramelized onions and pineapples. Jenny

had crab fries that were great, seasoned with something like

Tony's seasoning from back home, and you got a creamy

cheese dip with it.

At the airport we had one last cheesesteak at Chickie's

and Pete's, which is a local favorite. By the way, the Philly

cheesesteak was invented in the '30s by a hot dog vendor who

decided to do something different one day. So he made up the

first signature recipe Philly Cheesesteak and gave it to a

cabbie. All the cabbies fell in love with the sandwich, and,

well, the rest is history.

The Fans

We met a number of fans, grads from both the Army and Navy

academies, and even a few players, when I stormed the field

after Navy's missed field goal that was wide left at the last

second. Yep, hit the field again. Everywhere else it's called

"rush" the field, but with the cadets it's called "storm" the

field.

At around 1600 hours on Friday, Lt. Louis Rodriguez had informed us he intended to rendezvous with us for the battle between the Cadets of Army and the Midshipmen of Navy at 1400 hours the following day. Luis, or Lou Rod as I'm now calling him, our host for the TCU/West Virginia game in Week Seven, was in New York on a reconnaissance mission, and after clearing it with General Rodriquez, his wife, he was on go to engage in the stated mission.

Mick McDonnald, a '92 grad of West Point, brought it to our attention that this is a worldwide event watched by millions of servicemen and women all over the globe. Bret Pettus, a former Army player and '91 grad, said the teams he played on won three of four Army/Navy games, but the one they lost still haunts him.

The last group we skulled with was the Joint Operation Tailgate division, consisting of an equal number of Army and Navy grads, wives, and two tents, one for each Academy. They perceived us as enemy combatants at first. Hard looks were followed by an interrogation of who we were and what the hell

did we want. When they realized we were not begging for beer

like the last two interlopers, they became warm and approving

of our mission.

A Mr. McGowan noticed my LSU gear and asked if I

was familiar with the Seth Rewson story at LSU? I said no, and

he proceeded to tell me about a friend of his who served

overseas in harms way and then walked-on with the Tigers. He

became an inspiration to all of the LSU coaches and players

and was awarded a scholarship. If anyone's familiar with this

story let me know.

Then, we deployed into Lincoln Financial Field, home

of the NFC-leading Philadelphia Eagles, and staked our camp

under an overhang to stay dry and out of the, YES, FALLING

SNOW! Finally, I got my snow game. And, boy, did I get

snow, this was on the border of being a blizzard. During the

day of the game, it snowed five inches, and when I walked out

of my hotel first thing Saturday morning, I was like a kid

running around catching snowflakes on my tongue and

throwing snowballs. Jenny asked if I was a 10-year old, and I

said, "Today, probably so!"

At the stadium, in honor of the snow game, we were

able to capture club tickets which allowed us to go inside when

we wanted to and eat the great concessions I talked about. No

C-rations today! HOOAH!

THE GAME: "OK, BIG ED AND POPPA, NOW I GET IT!"

This game is like no other I've been to in my life. I always

thought big time programs had cornered the market on

traditions, but this rivalry is on another level. The pregame is

off the charts, with all the cadets from both academies

marching onto the field. Following their entrance, is a transfer

of seven cadets ceremoniously held at midfield. At the

beginning of their junior year, seven carefully chosen cadets

from both academies transfer to the opposite academy for one year. They become cadets for the other side for that year,

except during this game when they are transferred back for a

day. Then, the choirs from both academies gather together to

sing the national anthem in a half circle of harmonic

patriotism. The Army band is actually not made up of cadets,

but enlisted or commissioned members of the Army for whom

this is their full time job, and it has been this way for over two

hundred years.

Another remarkable tradition is the singing of each

others' alma mater after the game. The fan saying on both sides

is "Sing second!" because the losing team has to sing the other

team's alma mater first.

At halftime, whoever is present to represent the federal

government, either the President, Vice-President, Secretary of

State, etc., is transferred at midfield from one side to the other

by a group of senior cadets. They sit on one side the first half,

and are then transferred to the other side for the remaining half.

More modern politically correct stuff? No, been done this way forever.

There is another tradition that is rather interesting for Midshipmen. If Navy beats Army, in any sports program, a star is sewn onto their letterman jackets. Having that star is a prized possession.

The game began with Army easily driving for a TD, and I thought the rout was on. But, Navy responded with a drive of their own, scoring a field goal to make it 7-3 Army. As the game unfolded, I realized Army brought a bruising ground game and might not throw the ball the entire game. Meanwhile, the Navy quarterback seemed to run the ball on almost every play. I commented that at this rate he'd be dead by the 4th quarter. As the game wore on, Navy's quarterback made a 70-yard run in the 4th quarter. I joked, "Apparently all those runs aren't tiring him out cause he outran the defensive backs."

With about nine minutes left, Navy hung on to a 13-7

lead when Army's ground game came alive and went marching

through the snow like a white snowplow in their white

uniforms to honor the 10th Mountain Division, which I thought

was ironic considering the weather conditions. Navy wore a

cool blue-ish uniform which they said was to honor the Blue

Angels out of Pensacola.

With about five minutes left, Army finally scored and

with the extra point went ahead 14-13. Then, Navy proceeded

to sail slowly down the field until, with seconds left, they were

in position for a game winning field goal. But something

happened to remind us that we are all human. Two 5-yard

penalties cost Navy's field goal kicker precious yards that

resulted in him being out of his kicking comfort zone. He had

to kick from 48 yards out in a swirling snowstorm with only a

couple seconds left. The kick was up and long enough but wide

left. The Army cadets and Louis and Ed (sounds like an

expedition), stormed the field. The pure joy and happiness on

the faces of the Army cadets was priceless.

FINAL SCORE: ARMY 14, NAVY 13

As I put a wrap on the final regular season game, I reflect on

the unbelievable experience this has been. From the plains of

Stillwater, to the Valleys of Blacksburg, and State College, the

Indian Mounds of LSU, to the Oaks at Auburn, I've felt the

pulse of our country and find this is a wonderful country we

live in. Probably the best of this odyssey has been the people I

have met, and those I haven't even seen up close, but sat with

in stadiums across the country. I can't say enough about the

warmth and friendliness we have encountered, from sea to

shining sea! Was it coincidental that everyone we met was

gracious? Or, is it college football fans who are excited about

their team's chances that day, but who also feel the common

bond of the greatest sport? Did fate shine on us and that higher

being direct us each and every week to meet these hospitable folks? Or did they, as some I know did, just seek us out, immensely intrigued by our journey? For whatever reason, I wouldn't trade the people we met. Bill, Kim, Kenny, Louis, Bluegrass, Kevin, Sommer, Hal, Tony, David, and all the others, too many to name, have enriched my life and my understanding of human nature. Human nature in almost all of us is to be friendly and helping. It has never been more evident than what I have experienced during The Greatest Fall of All.

WINNERS AND LOSERS

Well, this week is hard since there weren't many games. but here it goes.

Winners

1) Army: After losing fourteen times in a row to Navy, Army has now started its own streak of 2. They sunk Navy with a ground game that reflects their heritage of ground warfare. To be truthful, however, Navy was a winner, too, because nobody is a loser in this game with the tradition, pageantry and

fellowship that I saw. Maybe I should say that we in America are the winners. To have the Cadets I met and observed as leaders and protectors of this nation, I can assure you we are in good hands.

2) Baker Mayfield: Crotch-grabbing and profanity aside, but not forgotten, Baker cooked-up a special season. It wasn't even close in the Heisman voting this year. The Rose Bowl is shaping up to be the Hell's Kitchen and Bulldog Whisperer show. Watch out Hollywood this will be the stuff of a movie to remember!

Losers

1) For the first time in fourteen weeks, I'm skipping this section. I'm feeling too inspired and happy to go there, so let's just say we were all winners this week and this year, and now it's time to get ready for Christmas and family. Oh, and Southern Heritage hams and turkeys, that's from my company if you didn't know. Have a great week, and we will be back in three weeks. But first, one more shout-out for everyone who

has made writing of this odyssey possible: my daughter, Savannah; my son, Eddie, and his girlfriend Meagan; and Glenn Roper; to all of them, I am thankful for their proof-reading and moral support. And last but not least, my beautiful college football-loving and patient wife, Jenny. She has supported this odyssey from the start and persevered through illness, fatigue, and me leaving my phone in four states, including Pennsylvania twice. But every time it has been misplaced, my phone shows back up like a cheap pair of sunglasses you can't lose. I think if I threw the phone out the window on the interstate, by the time I got home there would be somebody standing there saying, "Did you lose this?"

NEXT GAME: THE ROSE BOWL: GEORGIA VS. OKLAHOMA, JANUARY 1ST, 2018

This should be an instant classic. The Georgia bulldogs have only stumbled once, and they have looked the part of a national contender all year. After we saw the Oklahoma Sooners in

Week Two beat-down the eventual Big 10 champs, Ohio State,

we thought Baker Mayfield would probably win the Heisman,

and that Oklahoma would make the playoffs. We were right.

The SEC title game was the most predictable game of the year.

Last week, we alluded to the statistical advantage a loser seems

to have in a re-match and these Dawgs have been foaming at

the mouth to show the world they weren't as bad as they

looked in the first game. As far as the semi-final game in a

couple weeks, my son, Eddie, and his girlfriend, Meagan, are

going with us. We are looking forward to the Rose Parade, a

Lakers game, Disneyland, The Rose Bowl, and New Year's

Eve in California. I wanted to try something clever in that last

sentence, but there's a SCREAMING baby in front of me on

the plane, who hasn't stopped for forty-five minutes, and I

finally said to myself "Just finish the sentence, 'cause that poor

baby is giving me writer's cramp and a migraine."

HAPPY HOLIDAYS EVERYONE!

The Rose Bowl Parade

WEEK SIXTEEN: THE ROSE BOWL AND SEMI-FINAL CFP GAME

No. 2 OKLAHOMA VS. No. 3 GEORGIA

PASADENA, CALIFORNIA

JANUARY 1, 2018

NOTE: Sorry, readers, about the delayed report, but we had to

drive to Vegas on the 2nd, and I had severe headaches caused

by a combination of dry air, too much rich food, sensory

overload from craps and slot machines, and loud music from

shows. I know you're sympathetic about my health.

In the mid- to late 1800s many Americans in the Northeast and Midwest states migrated westward in search of better jobs, wider spaces, and milder weather. Many heard that California was the "Mediterranean of the West," blessed with mild winters and bountiful agricultural areas. Cities and towns were established and grew quickly.

Some of the more prominent residents of Pasadena, after its founding in 1856, formed a private social club called The Valley Hunt Club for men who were interested in hunting, fishing, gambling, and any other manly pursuits that wealthy dudes wished to pursue. Still in existence today, the club is so elitist it puts the "exclude" in the word exclusive. In 1890, at a club meeting, president Charles F. Holder, a Massachusetts zoology professor, said, "In New York, people are buried in snow, while here our flowers are blooming and our oranges about to bear. Let's hold a festival to show the world how wonderful our paradise is." With that, in 1890, The Tournament of Roses was born and a parade was held and games were

played.

There was no football yet, and the games included

ostrich races, bronco busting, and a race between an elephant

and a bulldog. The bulldog won, and, hmmm, I wonder if that's

a sign or an omen for this Georgia Bulldog team?

Ok, not really.

I was kidding. That race was between an elephant and a

camel, and the elephant won. Being of Lebanese descent, I

know something about camels, and the only way "Clyde"

could lose to an elephant, would be if he was drunk or bribed

with baklava.

In 1902, club members added a game called The East/

West Football Game in order to fund the Parade, which had

become immensely popular, and expensive. In the first game,

Michigan represented the East, and shot and de-feathered the

Stanford Cardinals, representing the West. The 49-0 win for

Michigan came after Stanford folded like a shot dove in the 3rd

quarter. They didn't just give up, lay down, and not play well

the rest of the game. They actually quit and walked off the field

and went home. I wonder if Clemson thought about that last

week after Alabama whipped 'em 24-6?

A few years later, the name of the football game was

changed to The Rose Bowl, and since it was the first bowl, it

has been forever called "The Grandaddy of Them All." I asked

some residents who had been to many Rose Bowls which game

was the greatest ever, and most said the 2006 game, when

Texas beat Southern California 41-38 on a last second TD run

by Texas QB Vince Young. I wonder if this game will live up

to the pregame hype, and maybe go down as one of the greatest

ever?

The Hype

Bulldogs vs. Sooners

The aerial attack vs. the ground troops

This is a monumental contest between two very powerful and well-coached teams. Both are peaking at the right time and enter this game with supreme confidence. Oklahoma's QB, Baker Mayfield, won the Heisman trophy and has been lauded in my reporting for his "highlight reel year" many times, dating back to Week Two.

The Sooners score more than Magic Mike, and are more cocky than a certain POTUS who tweets a lot. Georgia avenged their only loss by beating Auburn in the SEC championship, and will have the advantage in fans attending, with probably sixty-five percent of the crowd screaming for the Bulldogs. Georgia appears to be well-balanced on offense, defense, and they are also riding the momentum of a No. 1 early signing class of high school seniors to keep them in the National Championship hunt for years to come.

Both teams have been here once before, with Georgia winning in 1943, and Oklahoma winning in 2003. Georgia hasn't won the National Championship since 1980, but Oklahoma has won twice since then in 2000 and 1985. Ironically, my stepdaughter's grandfather on their dad's side, Jack Pounds, played for Georgia in the 1943 Rose Bowl when Georgia beat UCLA 9-0.

Although most sources list Notre Dame as the National Champion in 1943, Georgia felt slighted and claims the championship for that year. Jack's daughter, Carol Bowen, has been posting great old pics of Jack at the Rose Bowl festivities this past week on Facebook, including a picture of him with Rita Hayworth, Spencer Tracy, and Bob Hope.

Whoever wins this game will be just one win away from reaching the mountaintop of college football and being talked about seventy years from now like Jack's descendants.

The Sights

It would take two or three months to see all the top sights in the greater Los Angeles area, and we only had two days. But we covered a lot in that short period. When I think of LA, I think of Hollywood, Beverly Hills, and Disneyland. Hollywood, of course, is home to most of the film industry's production companies. Paramount, Warner Brothers, and Universal, all have great tours.

We went to a museum downtown that had a large and interesting collection of film artifacts, called the Max Factor Hollywood Museum. We checked out the Hollywood Walk of Fame, which is on both sides of Hollywood Boulevard for fifteen blocks, and Graumen's Chinese Theater, which has the footprints and handprints of many famous Hollywood stars. When I was here thirty years ago for the LSU/USC game, the tour guide told us to look for John Wayne's footprints. When I found them, I was shocked that such a large man could have worn such a small size 7 boot. When my son, Eddie, and his girlfriend, Meagan, found the footprints this trip, they thought

a midget must have been a stand-in for The Duke that day.

Beverly Hills is the home of Rodeo Drive, the most

expensive couple of shopping blocks west of Dubai. But the

real fun is being stared at in one of the exclusive stores while

guards look at you. Makes you feel like, "We hear your accent,

and know you're from the South, and you're about to ask how

much is that, so you obviously can't afford to be in here." It's

also fun to check out the cars going up and down the street all

day like fashion models, strutting to show the world how good-

looking they are, and how to wear with elegance a look of

smug indifference. Bugattis, Lamborghinis, Rolls-Royces,

Ferraris, and the like roll by all day long one after another.

Eddie said, "Do you realize in the past five minutes about

thirty or forty million dollars worth of cars has passed by?"

Expensive doesn't begin to describe this place. As we

walked by a watch shop, I only saw two watches in the store,

and a couple, maybe Southerners, asked the price of the watch on the left. When they got an answer, the man said, "Oh,

twenty thousand, that's not bad." The salesman replied, "I said

two HUNDRED thousand." That must be one hell of a smart

watch. Too smart for a Southerner. But, who knows, maybe it

makes coffee, predicts pony races and creates bitcoin.

If you think the buildings are made of gold, you'd be

partially right. Beverly Hills City Hall has a gold-trimmed

cupola dating back to the 1930s.

A trip to Santa Monica is well worth the 45-minute ride

to see The Pier, the original Muscle Beach, and all the great

seafood restaurants. Santa Monica Pier, made famous in many

movies, is like a boardwalk with rides, shops, musicians, and

places to fish. Meagan said she had played an Xbox game that

involved all the attractions on the pier. If you want to relax and

people-watch the beautiful people, the Santa Monica Pier is the

place. It's also melting pot-USA, with many nationalities, and

foreign languages on display.

The Rose Parade is not easy to put into words. We stayed at a hotel on the parade route which is five-and-a-half miles long and we had front row seats on the curb. We were further down the route, however, and I watched the first few floats described in detail on TV, before it showed up out front.

The amount of time and diversity of materials that go into each float is nothing short of remarkable. It is not unusual for 40,000 man hours, and some 200 different kinds of flora to be used on each float. Watching the beginning of the parade on television, the announcer gave details I would not have known from my curbside viewing. Powdered fruit, flowers from Africa, oranges, pomegranates, blueberries, and tea leaves, are just a few of the examples of hundreds of fruits and flora that go into a float. The Rose Parade is definitely a bucket list item, since it is one of the oldest and most colorful traditions in our country. We were amazed to see families camping out twenty-four hours before the parade began, many with kids sleeping on the concrete with just a blanket wrapped around them, fighting off the 43-degree weather all night. I asked one family

why they set -up so early and was told it was their third

generation to do this, a family tradition for decades. And, the

125th Rose Bowl Parade rolled on, creating new family

traditions as it went, I'm sure.

The Food

Well, obviously greater LA is such a large area, the food

options are too numerous to list. But I'll hit some highlights.

Our great Penn State buddy, Bill Kohl, is here on

business a lot, and being on the National Restaurant

Association Board, he is friends with many of the great chefs

and restaurant owners in America. He recommended Spago in

Beverly Hills, Pie and Burger in Pasadena, and Waterfront

Grill in Santa Monica.

We went to Wolfgang Puck's famous Spago first, and

we asked if Wolfgang was there since he and Bill Kohl are

friends, and Wolfgang's company president. Unfortunately, he wasn't in the restaurant, but when we told the waiter of our connection, and about the blog, he made sure we had a memorable experience. The service was impeccable and the food was worthy of another visit. Although I heard from one friend who felt for whatever reason that Spago was an overpriced tourist trap, we had an exceptional meal. Among the many delicacies we tried were Big Eye Tuna, Spanish Octopus, Venison Ravioli, Veal Porterhouse, Snake River Wagyu Steak, Black Bass and Chocolate Inspiration.

For lunch the next day, we went to ESPN's College GameDay favorite, Pie and Burger. A hole in the wall sort of place, Pie and Burger has become one of the most well-known breakfast and lunch places in all of LA. Michael Osborne, the current owner, ate at Pie and Burger as a 9-year old in 1963 when it opened. As a USC, student Michael worked there and eventually bought Pie and Burger. The rest is history. Pie and Burger has been named one of the five best burgers in America by Food Network. But that's not even the most impressive thing. The list of pies and cakes is incredible! There's

Boysenberry, and the rare Olallieberry pies, which are the most

popular. Meringue pies, fruit pies, and fresh cakes, all made hot

and fresh in the kitchen, are to die for.

Mike, a '76 USC grad, said he's seen many great Rose

Bowls, but the greatest was the previously mentioned 2006

game when his Trojans lost to Texas. Mike said, "I haven't

been able to extricate that stake from my heart yet!" As we

were leaving, Mike said, "Hang around, Lee Corso and the

College GameDay crew will be here in fifteen minutes." I said.

"So GameDay even follows us for dining. Sorry, Mike, but

we've got a tight schedule."

On New Year's Eve night, we ate at the old Pasadena

hip spot, Barney's Beanery. It originally opened in West

Hollywood in 1920, and over the years has become a favorite

for actors, producers, rock and roll legends, and artists. With

three floors, and an immense collection of rock and roll

memorabilia, it's worth your time to pay a visit. And, the food is good! They have a newspaper-style menu with 100

selections, and the place is easy to find on old Route 66 in Old

Town Pasadena. So, go "Get your kicks on Route 66." I

wonder if anyone younger than 66 got that one, my reference

here to the old TV series from the '60s?

The famous Route 66 starts in Chicago, and ends in

Santa Monica at the Pier. Over the years, it's been called the

"Mother Road" and symbolizes Americans freedom to travel,

and our quest to look for adventure on the road. Sort of like

me, on this football road trip odyssey.

I can't leave the food section without mentioning In-N-

Out burger. I've been hearing about this franchise for decades,

and it became for me a sort of urban legend, since there were

no locations in the Southern U.S., and, yes, man always wants

what he doesn't have. So, when I picked up Eddie and Meagan

from the LA airport, he said all he could think about was In-N-

Out Burger. Always heard it was famous and Eddie seemed

adamant about trying it out. So we pretty quickly found one

and ordered. Although Eddie insisted he liked his burger, Meagan and I agreed that the Food Network would list the eatery in the bottom five burger places in America. Plus, the shake tasted like melted Blue Bunny ice cream. Not Blue Bell, mind you, which is the best ice cream, but the wanna-be ice cream brand. Our food was so bad that when Meagan and I threw both our burgers and shakes into a dumpster, a stray dog ran when he saw the bag and wrappers with the In-N-Out logo! Now I know why they call the place In-N-Out. It goes out as fast as it went in.

From LA cuisine's "Good-Stuff" column, we have to sing the praises of Randy's Donuts. You know the sign, a huge donut on top of the store that's been seen in a hundred movies. I had to go try 'em, and I'm pleased to say they were fresh, warm, and absolute top-shelf. Four stars for their creative offerings, and the HUGE glazed donut Jenny tried to eat. Of course the only five-star donut place in the world is still Tat-O-Nut Donut Shop in Ocean Springs, Mississippi. Their delicious hot donuts are made with potato flour, and are so good wrecks

happen outside the shop when the line of people trying to get

inside spills into the street.

This is where I usually write about the tailgate food, but

since ninety percent of the fans flew in for the game, tailgating

was sparse at best. We decided to try anyway, and were warmly

received by the fans smoking weed, getting high for the game.

When a Georgia fan said the Bulldogs would win by 30, I

asked what he was smoking. He answered without hesitation,

"Blue Boy Bud. The bud tender recommended it. Want a hit?"

Seems California picked this day to legalize recreational

marijuana and the fans were stoking and smoking like Cheech

and Chong. At least three tailgaters offered us beer, food or pot.

The Game

The fans did not seem as intense as at some of the rival games

we saw this year. They engaged each other in conversation,

talked about which team they hated, and said cordially, "May the best team win." I, on the other hand, had to pull for

Georgia, since they are in the same clan as my team, LSU.

Most games this year I've been neutral while wearing my LSU

gear and have been warmly received everywhere. But if I had

any doubts about who I was rooting for, those doubts drifted

away like so much blue haze before the game, when two

separate groups of Oklahoma fans, upon seeing my LSU

apparel, yelled "Go Notre Dame!" The Irish were playing LSU

that same day. Guess Oklahoma's still mad about losing to

LSU in the 2003 National Championship game. Oklahoma fans

seemed to mirror their QB Baker Mayfield's cockiness, while

Georgia fans were cautiously optimistic. They've had their

hopes dashed so many times before.

The seats were the tightest I've ever seen with no more

than seven or eight inches from the front of your seat to the

back of the chair back in front of you. We all had to turn our

legs sideways to fit. Yes, even worse than Wisconsin's

munchkin seats. Guess those Valley Hunt people(the club that started this Rose Bowl), were Smurfs. Then, during the

singing of the national anthem, which always gets me, the

mother of all fly-bys occurred. A B-2 Stealth Bomber with its

bat-like design appeared on the horizon, and seemed to slowly

float over the stadium. It was VERY low, and jaws dropped as

the stadium shook and everyone looked around in amazement.

Coolest fly-by ever!

When the game began, Oklahoma took their first

possession and stormed down the field for an easy TD. Georgia

answered with a Sony Michel 13-yard reception and run to tie

it. But after that, it got ugly as Oklahoma outscored the Dawgs

24 points to 7 points. Then, with only six seconds left in the

first half, and leading 31-14 for a cruise to a blowout win,

something inexplicable happened. Oklahoma's first year coach,

Lincoln Riley, made a rookie mistake. Brain fart would be

kind, but this decision was dumber than betting on buggy

races. He called for an onside kick! Georgia recovered, and

kicked a 55-yard field goal, the longest in Rose Bowl history, and seized back the momentum. As the second half unfolded,

a buzz like electricity hummed through the stadium and a high-

voltage charge energized the Bulldogs, as each new play

seemed to heighten a momentum shift. As the third quarter

unfolded, it became apparent the field goal before the half had

given Georgia new life, and by the fourth quarter the game was

tied 31-31.

Georgia continued their onslaught, going ahead 38-31

in the fourth. I looked at Eddie and said, "If Baker Mayfield is

to cement his legend, now's the time!" And Baker got in the

kitchen cooked up a timely drive and an 11-yard TD pass to

even the score again at 38. On the very next Georgia

possession they fumbled, and Oklahoma picked up the fumble

and ran in for a TD with only 6:52 left. The Dawg fans around

us were deflated and looked like guys who were just taunted,

"You're back in timeout again. Did you really think you were

gonna finally get to the top?"

But then a funny thing happened on the way to time out. Georgia hunkered down and drove for the tying score with fifty-five seconds left. Overtime!! In the first overtime game in Rose Bowl history, the teams swapped field goals and led to a second overtime! Georgia kept Oklahoma out of the end zone, and blocked Oklahoma's field goal attempt. Now, all Georgia had to do was score. Most people thought the Bulldogs would play conservative and opt for a field goal, but the senior Sony Michel would have none of that, and he ran 27 yards for a TD, and into Georgia lore forever. What a game! Every Dawg fan around us said it was the greatest game they'd ever witnessed. Eddie was in full agreement. A Georgia fan from Palisades, California, who sat beside his wife, said it was the greatest day of his life. I asked, "What about your wedding? He looked at his wife and said, "Sorry honey, but this is No. 1." I have tried in all my reporting to explain this college football fan thing. Here was a perfect example!

Now Kirby Smart and his resilient Georgia Bulldogs

are on to Atlanta for a classic matchup between Smart and his

former boss, Nick Saban, and a shot at Alabama for the crown.

FINAL SCORE: GEORGIA 54, OKLAHOMA 48

NEXT WEEK'S GAME:

THE NATIONAL CHAMPIONSHIP IN HOT 'LANTA,

GEORGIA

Well, I can't believe it's almost over. Week Seventeen is upon

us, and the odyssey ends where it started. The Mercedes-Benz

Stadium was brand new on Week One when we saw Bama

destroy Florida State, a beating the Seminoles never recovered

from.

Now, an emotionally drained Bulldog team has to come

back somehow and beat the 500-pound gorilla we know as

Alabama. But, don't count the Dawgs out. It will be a pro-

Bulldog crowd, and they have a lot of seniors who don't want to be denied.

If Bama wins, this game will cement Saban's place in college football history as the greatest coach ever with six National Championships, five of them in the last nine years. Unprecedented is the word you're looking for. This is expected to be a good old-fashioned Southern defensive slobber knocker. And that's why I'm taking the overs which are 46. Which means I think more than 46 total points will be scored. Watch out for more scoring than you think. It may be a 31-28 game. Let's get this party started!

A fitting tribute to our nation and "The Greatest Fall of All"

WEEK SEVENTEEN: THE NATIONAL CHAMPIONSHIP
NO. 3 GEORGIA VS. NO. 4 ALABAMA

MERCEDES-BENZ STADIUM

ATLANTA, GEORGIA

The winner of this epic battle will forever be called the

National Champion of college football for 2017. But the path

to claiming a National Championship in college football has

not always been this clear-cut.

The College Football Playoff started in 2014, and this year marks the fourth year that four teams enter into a playoff with semi-finals whose winners play for the championship. Before that there was a two-team championship game from 1998 to 2013. According to the results of both these systems, there were only minor controversies and an occasional tweak in the system.

But before 1998 there were certain years when multiple teams "claimed" to be the national champs from some teams whose arguments were dubious at best. For instance, Alabama claims sixteen National Championships before this game, but according to the official NCAA website Bama has eight undisputed titles, and shares seven. Among the shared titles are some teams whose claims were not supported by the most acknowledged polls and sources at the time. From 1936 to today, the AP (Associated Press) Poll, which is the newspaper sports writers' poll, was usually accepted as the most reliable. The UPI (United Press International) Coaches Poll was not as widely recognized because most coaches admitted they were

too busy to know what "Coach X or O was doing with his

Jimmys and Joes."

If you want to see what REAL stretches on claims to

titles are, check out Princeton and Yale who claim 28 and 27

titles, respectively. Anyway, now the Champion as determined

in our CFP playoff system is universally accepted. Except for

the University of Central Florida currently claims to be champs

on the basis of their 13-0 record, and have put up a billboard in

Tuscaloosa challenging Alabama to a fight. RIGHT! And that

fight would be mercy-called in the first round. This game

would be like Mike Tyson vs. Danny Devito.

The Hype

Would it be an understatement to say this game needs no hype?

Sixteen weeks ago we began postulating that this football

season would be the greatest fall of all. Intersectional games,

rivalries, conference championships, and bowl games would

lead to the ultimate semi-finals, and the most exciting

championship ever played.

How did I know this, without knowing *this exact*

outcome?

Because I would be part of the entire process, and not a

bystander. Therefore, to me and my readers who were with me

the entire way, we would experience the season as never

before. And boy did we! Sights, food, interesting people, and

emotionally charged fans and games were ours to enjoy every

week. Now we are at the end, and it ends where it started, at

the Mercedes-Benz Stadium in Atlanta.

Alabama had a great season, no doubt, but the stars had

to line up and have Ohio State beat an undefeated Wisconsin

team in the Big 10 championship for them to get in as the

fourth seed. Everything clicked, and Vegas immediately

installed Mr. Congeniality's team as the favorite. Georgia, who had to win an emotionally-charged double overtime game at

the Rose Bowl, may be drained.

As I have mentioned many times before, Georgia fans

feel vindicated for forcing their old coach out, but they can't

bark till they've won it all. The last time Georgia was this

close, Bama dashed their hopes by barely beating the Dawgs in

the SEC Championship in 2012. The powers to be, the Football

Selection Committee, isn't happy about the lack of diversity

representing the sport, with two SEC teams in the final.

Rumors are they may appeal it to a California court and get

Grambling and Carlisle Indian School to play for the National

Championship.

This game is not just about this year, it's also about

whether a new guard is taking over. Georgia's new coach,

Kirby Smart, came from a highly successful turn as the

defensive coordinator at Alabama, and he appears to be a

Saban clone, just happier and more congenial. Georgia is fresh

off a No. 1 recruiting class and the future is so bright the

Dawgs are buying Ray Ban stock! I only hope this game is as

exciting as the Rose Bowl, but I wouldn't count on overtime

again.

The Sights

In Week One and Week Fifteen, I described The College

Football Hall Of Fame, the Georgia Aquarium, the CNN

Center and the Fox Theater, so refer back to those weeks if

you're heading to Hot 'Lanta. You might also consider the

World of Coca-Cola, Six Flags Over Georgia, Underground

Atlanta, and the Georgia State Capitol.

The World of Coca-Cola is a museum dedicated to the

history of the world's most recognizable brand. It is located

just a couple of blocks from the exact spot where John

Pemberton created the original formula. The museum allows

you to taste sixty different flavors of soda pop from around the

world and is very kid friendly.

Six Flags was originally built in 1967 as one of the three Six Flags theme parks in the country. Among their roller coasters are Mind Bender and Goliath, both top-ranked by Amusement Today. Hurricane Harbor is a 7-acre water park that was just added in 2014.

On my first visit to Atlanta, I remember visiting Underground Atlanta and thinking how cool the place was. With shopping and entertainment galore, it was one of America's best known places after it opened in 1969. I saw Atlanta Rhythm Section play one night in a club there and told a friend they needed to quit playing their own music and just do covers because they'd never make it with their original stuff. Within two years, ARS had numerous Top 20 hits, played with every top rock band around, and also played in the White House. Mr. Music Critic here is writing a football blog while those guys are still raking in the royalties. Alas, all good things usually come to an end, and the Underground has been sold for development into more residential and retail spaces and is

closed during construction.

The Georgia State Capitol, located in downtown

Atlanta, is built in the Neoclassical style of the U.S. Capitol,

and is one of the most beautiful state capitols in the country.

The dome is gilded with native gold leaf from Lumpkin

County, Georgia, where, ironically, the very first American

Gold Rush took place in the 1830s. There are a number of tour

companies offering very inexpensive and informative tours of

the Capitol.

The Food

This week the food section is not going to blow your skirt up.

Jenny and I only got back from out west a day before the

National Championship game and had to leave the day after to

get back to work. In Week Fifteen, I talked about the hot spots

in Atlanta for dining and covered it pretty well.

I must thank my wonderful neighbor, Kay Evans, for

inviting us to stay at her condo in Atlanta. Kay's condo is on

Peachtree Road in the upscale Buckhead area, described as the

Beverly Hills of the East with its mansions and expensive

shops. Buckhead is also home to almost all of Georgia's

billionaires, along with Elton John, Tyler Perry and many hip-

hop or rap artists whose names I'd have to get from Eddie.

People like Lil Wayne, Lil Pump, Lil Pumpkin and Lil I Wear

Lots of Chains. Thanks again Kay, your place is beautiful and

convenient.

When my friend, John McMillan, suggested after Week

One in Atlanta that I write more about the tailgating here, I

explained there wasn't any. Once again, if there were tailgates

with people partying and cooking, they must have been out of

sight in Underground Atlanta. But since I reported on my visits

to Alabama's campus, and tailgaters at the Auburn/Georgia

game, then you know why Southern tailgating is the best.

The Game

First, I have to address the ticket situation and how that worked

out. Two weeks before the game the cheapest ticket on Stubhub

was $2,400 in the nosebleed end zone. That is by far the

highest ticket price I saw listed this entire year. Two days

before the game, prices had "dropped" to $1,300 per ticket, and

I felt, based on the prior sixteen weeks' experience, that I could

find a ticket at the game for $600-800 each. Still a lot of

money, but after all I've been through, I wasn't backing down

on the last game.

So we parked about a mile from the stadium, walked to

the front of the College Football Hall of Fame and began

scouting. After thirty minutes of striking out, I finally saw two

guys sell two tickets to a couple before I could get over to

them. I still asked the dude if he had anymore, and he said yes.

When I asked him the price, he said $1,500. I jokingly asked if

that was for the pair. When he replied yes, I said to Jenny, "Just

what I thought, prices are coming down." Prices are lower than

Stubhub, and the cold, rainy and windy weather is keeping

potential buyers away. Damn I'm smart!

Before I could say ok, he said, "Just give me $1200."

Warning bells went off in my head. and I looked at him and

said, "You came down too fast. I've been doing this my whole

life, and you're making me wonder about the credibility of

these tickets." He and his partner assured me they are on this

corner every Falcons game. Then, he called me from his cell

phone so I'd have his number. I still felt concerned, but I didn't

see any other options. So I gave him the money and Jenny and

I headed to the Fan Fest. When we presented our tickets to the

lady at the Fan Fest entrance, she said "For some reason these

tickets aren't scanning." My heart sank like the Poseidon when

another lady checked the numbers on the tickets, and she said,

"I'm sorry, but these are counterfeit."

I let loose an angry, broken-hearted string of profanity.

I was going to type all those characters for cuss words, but, I

might get tears in my eyes again.

We ran back and of course the guys were gone. I told a policeman in a car parked right where we bought the tickets and his response was "Sorry, good luck." So now we really were worried. Here we were at the last game, and I've got to get in. This is the grand finale to the whole odyssey. But, there were no tickets anywhere. We went back to the stadium and separated so we could both look for tickets, but after an hour, the only tickets were standing-room-only for $2000 each. And I didn't have that much cash on me anymore.

Just when I was about to start looking to spend my money on Valium or Xanax, two middle age guys on mini foldable bikes, like the kind Shriners ride in parades, passed by and said "You looking for two?"

"Hell yeah," I replied. "$...," he said.

Nope. I'm not gonna tell you how much, 'cause my father would come out of his grave. So I said, "Ok, but I don't have that much cash."

He said, "What about cash and a check?" Well, my checkbook was in the car one mile away, and it would take a long time in this cold rain and gusty wind to get there and back. So he said, "Take my bike." Picture a bike a four-year-old would ride, a thing that collapses into something you could put in a grocery bag, and you've got it. It was raining harder now, the winds were gusting 20-25 mph, the streets were slick, the one mile back is up and down hills, and this guy insisted I go back and get my checkbook. Now, I cycle a lot but this was like asking a race car driver to race a go-cart in a mud derby through a hurricane! Could this get any worse?

So I got on it and started to take off, and he said, "Oh yeah, I almost forgot to tell you, the steering is very shaky, oh, and the brakes don't work."

Off I went, and he wasn't joking about the brakes and steering. But, somehow I got to the car and back without wrecking. Freezing and soaked, we concluded our transaction and Jenny and I headed to the gates. While waiting in line for forty-five minutes, we told people around us about the

counterfeit tickets. Then some guy said, "Let me see the last

tickets you bought." He informed us these might be counterfeit

also because they didn't look like any other tickets he'd seen.

We stopped breathing. When we finally got to the ticket

scanner, the tickets didn't scan. She tried it again, and on the

third try it finally worked and we were in. The final cost of

tickets for this game was more than the cost of ALL the tickets

combined for the entire year. If the game itself is any more

nerve wracking than this, I'm in trouble. I don't know if I

could take it.

And, of course, the game WAS nerve wracking! And, of

course, I made it. How could I not, after all this?

The first half belonged to Georgia, as they took a 13-0

lead and out-gained Bama by more than a hundred yards.

Bama's QB, Jalen Hurts, was throttled by the Georgia defense,

and it appeared it would become a Georgia blowout. But at the beginning of the second half, coach Nick Saban, switched QBs

and put in the second string QB, Tua Tagovailoa. We'll just call

him Tua to make it easier on the typist.

Up until now Tua was best known as the subject of a

hilarious call on an XM Radio sports show, when a Bama

caller asked how did the coaches communicate with him when

he played. When asked what did he mean, the caller said,

"Well, he's from Hawaii, so how do the coaches communicate

with him." And the caller was dead serious!

Jenny said she gave credit to Saban for making a smart

call to switch QBs, but I don't think he had any choice. If he

didn't do something to shake things up, his offense wouldn't

have moved. It's what you do in sports. It's next man up. In

baseball, you put in a new pitcher, and it throws the other team

off balance. And Tua definitely threw the Georgia defense off

balance.

As the second half progressed, you could see Bama gaining confidence and momentum every minute. As the game wound down, I told Jenny if Georgia doesn't score again, they're toast. Momentum is a funny dynamic in football. For sixty years I've both played and watched football and, although it doesn't make sense, momentum exists as a reckoning force on the field. How many times have we seen one team completely dominate another, and then something happens to lift the others' spirits, and the teams reverse roles and the loser becomes the winner?

As the fourth quarter dwindled down to seven minutes left, Tua led Bama on a drive to Georgia's six-yard line. On fourth and four, Tua threw into a crowd of players, but, Bama's Calvin Ridley came away with it in the end zone tying the score at 20-20. Then Bama made an important stop forcing Georgia to punt. With 2:55 left Bama takes over on their own 35-yard line. Tua proceeds to march Bama to Georgia's 16-yard line. With 3 seconds left, Bama's place kicker

Pappanastos missed a 35-yard field goal and time expired.

OVERTIME AGAIN!

But, then in overtime, we found out it just wasn't

Georgia's day. The Dawgs went first, and were held out of the

end zone, and had to kick a very long field goal just to score!

Now it was Bama's turn. Score a TD on their series of

downs, and they win. Kick a field goal, it's tied, and we go to

the second overtime. Score nothing and Georgia wins. On the

very first play, Bama's second string freshman QB Tua is

sacked for a giant loss, and now it appears the best they can do

is have Pappanastos try another field goal. We couldn't see

him, but I guessed he was at that time throwing up and being

counseled by the team psychologist. He was saved from the

gut-wrenching pressure, though, when Tua put it all on the line

and went for the end zone and they scored for the winning TD!

Wide receiver Devonta Smith, a Louisiana native, caught the

winning TD and will forever be remembered in Alabama

football lore. Its incomprehensible to me how you let a wide receiver get behind you in those circumstances. You keep him in front of you, and let him have a shorter pass, but, it's inexcusable to let your man get five yards past you. This is football, though, and as we've said before, unpredictable things can happen with 18- to 22-year-old men.

So, Saban cements himself as the greatest college football coach ever after winning five National Championships in the last nine years. Sorry Bear, slide over and make room on your seat in the front of the Bama Bus.

FINAL SCORE: ALABAMA 26, GEORGIA 23

NEXT WEEK: REST, OH SWEET REST! AND SOME AWESOME REFLECTION.

I find myself in a bittersweet moment now. It's like I finished a marathon, and I am thrilled that I did what I first set out to do over four months ago. But another part of me is going to miss writing these weekly reports, meeting the unbelievable people we've met, and experiencing this adventures of a lifetime.

Hard to put a "wrap" on something so defining and full of hope

for me. Hope for our kids, hope for our country, and hope for

life. The things I have witnessed and the people I've met have

shown me we still live in the greatest country ever, and don't

let any news media tell you otherwise.

I thought, before we wind it up, it might be fun to give some

awards for the year so here goes.

BEST UNIVERSITY EXPERIENCE: Notre Dame. The

employees treated us like rock stars and made us wanna attend

at least one ND game a year. They said they are saving our

special seats for us, and I appreciate the 1988 replica ring.

Thanks, Hal!

SINGLE BEST TAILGATE: Penn State's Bill Kohl and Ken

Rapp, and the rest of their crew. Sometimes in life, if you

venture out of your comfort zone, you get lucky and meet

people who become your friends for life, who enhance your

being, people you'd like to have known your whole life, and

that's Bill and Ken. The tailgate with its Tomahawk steaks,

lump crab meat, Kobe burgers, and assortment of other

delicacies was the single best! But the friendship we developed

went well beyond their hospitality.

MOST EXCITING GAME: Three to choose from: 1) The

National Championship game. 2) The Rose Bowl. 3) The Iron

Bowl. All were intense, loud, and had season-defining

moments for the winning team, but I have to choose The Rose

Bowl. Two overtimes in what might be the greatest Rose Bowl

ever, and a Georgia team I was pulling for who came back

from a 17-point deficit—it was all too exhilarating.

BEST UNIVERSITY FAMILY: The Kevin Henry family

from Auburn. Kevin, who I sat next to and enjoyed talking to at

the Auburn/Georgia game in Auburn, is the head of a special

university family. Since he has three daughters and is outvoted

regularly, lets give him the "head" designation. Kevin played

baseball for Auburn with Bo Jackson, and his wife, Meg, was a gymnast at Auburn. His oldest daughter, Sommer, who

graduated was a cheerleader for Auburn. His middle daughter,

Shea, is a cheerleader at Auburn now, and his youngest

daughter Shea has been asked to be a cheerleader at Auburn

next year. So, in addition to thanking him for giving us the Iron

Bowl tickets we must applaud him and his wonderful family

for being the Best University Family.

MOST BEAUTIFUL STADIUM & BEST GUIDE/HOST:

Luis Rodriguez and TCU's Amon G. Carter Stadium. The

stadium is also called "Hell's Half Acre." When the designers

were thinking about how to build this stadium, they were told

to make it the Camden Yards of college football, a reference to

the beautiful Baltimore Orioles baseball stadium. It is

architecturally alluring, if not large. Luis hosted us, guided us,

introduced us to major TCU athletic people and even met us

later in the year for the Army/Navy game. If he doesn't run for

mayor of Fort Worth, it's a waste of talent.

GAME WITH THE BEST TRADITIONS: Army/Navy. The

Cadets and Midshipmen with their stately uniforms, and great

traditions, coupled with a blizzard made for an epic football

game. One for the ages.

BEST TAILGATING UNIVERSITY: Not being a homer

here, I promise. LSU, without a doubt, and hands-down.

Because of the cultural differences, LSU tailgaters take more

pride in cooking at their tailgates, and you're talking 200,000

people on campus for a big game. Gumbo, jambalaya, étouffée,

Boudin sausage, and crawfish pasta, are among the many

South Louisiana dishes you just won't see at any other football

tailgates. The single best dish I had this year, and we had a lot,

was the "whaler" soft shell crabs that had just been caught that

morning and fried in front of us. The cook said, "They slept in

the bay last night."

MOST LOYAL READERS OF MY BLOG: Tonyia Tonore,

Hugh Coachman, and Carol Bowen. All three supported and

encouraged me each and every single week. They, along with

so many others, have given me the compliments that made me want to try and improve the reports each week, and the strength to keep on going despite a destroyed knee, numerous infections, jet lag, car lag, and mental and physical fatigue. Thanks to everyone who read and enjoyed "our" blog.

When I initially set out on this odyssey, it was to honor my father. Of course, being a lifelong college football fan myself, I knew it would be the experience of a lifetime. What I didn't anticipate, however, were the lessons I'd learn along the way. First, I learned that the vast majority of people you meet in life are good people, and they are often very generous and more willing to help than you might think. Second, I learned that all true college football fans share a deep passion for their team and cherish their own time-honored traditions. Next, I learned that everyone has a story. Whether it is football related or not, everyone has a valuable perspective and unique experiences to share. Lastly, as Nike says, "Just do it." "It" goes by different names: bucket list, dream list, or wish list.

Regardless of what you may call it, now is the time to do "it."

Take a leap of faith and trust that everything will turn out okay

in the end.

And now it comes to an end. Where did this lump in

my throat come from? I'm looking out the window of my

second floor living room at the Spanish moss-covered 300-

year-old live oak tree in my yard, *and thinking how lucky I am*

to have experienced this, The Greatest Fall of All!

The Greatest Fall of All Recipes

Week One
Alabama vs. Florida State
Atlanta, Georgia

Reuben Sandwich
Fun Fact: Arnold Reuben (1883-1970), the founder of Reuben's Restaurant and Delicatessen in New York City, remembers that her father made the first Reuben Sandwich in 1914.

Late one evening a leading lady of actor Charlie Chaplin came into the restaurant and said, "Reuben, make me a sandwich, make it a combination, I'm so hungry I could eat a brick." He took a loaf of rye bread, cut two slices on the bias and stacked one piece with sliced Virginia ham, roast turkey, and imported Swiss cheese, topped it off with coleslaw and lots of Reuben's special Russian dressing and the second slice of bread. He served it to the lady who said, "Gee, Reuben, this is the best sandwich I ever ate, you ought to call it the Annette Seelos Special." To which he replied, "Like hell I will, I'll call it a Reuben's Special."

Another version is Reuben Kulakofsky (1873-1960), a wholesale grocer in Omaha, Nebraska and co-owner of Central Market there from 1900 to 1943, created the Reuben Sandwich. Kulakofsky belonged to a weekly poker group whose members apparently enjoyed fixing their own sandwiches every bit as much as they enjoyed playing poker. One of the players, Charles Schimmel, owner of the Blackstone Hotel in Omaha, put the Reuben Sandwich on the hotel menu. The sandwich seems to have been a collaborative effort by all the players.

1/2 cup Russian Dressing (see recipe below)*
6 slices marble rye bread
1/2 pound thinly-sliced corned beef
1/4 pound thinly-sliced Swiss cheese
1 cup well-drained sauerkraut
Butter

Spread the prepared Russian Dressing on one side of each bread slice, then layer corned beef, Swiss cheese, and sauerkraut on 3 slices of the prepared Bread. Place the remaining prepared bread slices over the top of each sandwich.

In a large frying pan over low heat, melt some butter. Add the prepared sandwiches and slowly grill the sandwiches until nicely browned, using a bacon press to weigh it down. Add additional butter and gently turn sandwiches and brown on the other side. Remove from heat, cut sandwiches in half, and serve immediately.

Traditionally Reuben Sandwiches are served with a large dill pickle slice.
Makes 3 Reuben Sandwiches.

Russian Dressing Recipe:
1/2 cup good-quality mayonnaise
2 tbsp ketchup
1 tsp Worcestershire sauce
1 tsp prepared horseradish
Freshly cracked pepper
Pinch of cayenne pepper
Salt to taste

In a bowl, combine mayonnaise, ketchup, Worcestershire Sauce, horseradish, pepper, cayenne pepper, and salt. Adjust according to taste. Refrigerate any unused dressing

Week Two
Oklahoma vs. Ohio State
Columbus, Ohio

Supreme Mac'n Cheese
8 tbsp unsalted butter (1 stick divided)
1 cup panko breadcrumbs
8 oz elbow macaroni
1/2 small sweet onion, diced
1/4 cup all-purpose flour
2 cups whole milk
1 cup heavy cream
1 tsp kosher salt
1 tsp dried mustard
1/2 tsp fresh ground black pepper
1/2 tsp grated nutmeg
1/4 cup sriracha garlic sauce (this can be adjusted to taste)
1 3/4 cups shredded sharp cheddar cheese
1/3 cup grated parmigiano-reggiano cheese

Preheat oven to 400 degrees. Lightly spritz a 2-quart casserole dish with nonstick cooking spray.

In a large saucepan over medium heat, melt 4 tbsp of the butter. Add the bread crumbs, stirring gently. Turn off the heat, allow the bread crumbs to absorb the butter and reserve.
In a large stockpot, bring 2 quarts of salted water to a rolling boil. Add the macaroni noodles and stir. Cook until the noodles are just slightly undercooked, 7 to 8 minutes.

While the pasta is cooking, melt the remaining 4 tbsp of butter in a large saucepan over medium heat. Add the onion and cook, stirring occasionally, until the onion begins to sweat, about 5 minutes. Whisk in the flour. Cook for 2-3 minutes, stirring constantly to avoid lumps. Add 1/2 cup of milk while whisking. Once the milk has been absorbed by the flour and thickened slightly, add the remainder of the milk, followed by the cream. Add the salt, dried mustard, pepper, and nutmeg. Simmer gently for 5 minutes, stirring occasionally.

Stir in the Sriracha. Gradually add 1 1/2 cups of the cheddar while slowly whisking, one handful at a time. Once all the cheese has melted, toss in the cooked macaroni, coating the noodles with the cheese sauce. Transfer the noodles and sauce to the baking dish. Top with the parmigiano-reggiano cheese and the remaining 1/4 cup cheddar cheese. Cover with an even layer of the buttered bread crumbs.

Bake, uncovered, until golden brown, 18 to 22 minutes. Allow to sit for 5 minutes so the molten cheese lava can cool just a touch. Divide into squares, place, and garnish with parsley.

Week Three
Clemson vs. Louisville
Louisville, Kentucky

Big Brown Hotel: Hot Brown
14 oz sliced roasted turkey breast
2 slices thickly sliced bread, crusts trimmed, toasted
4 slices cooked bacon
2 Roma tomatoes, sliced into halves
Chopped parsley

Melt butter in a 2-quart saucepan. Whisk in flour until combined. Cook until a thick paste (roux) forms. Continue cooking 2 minutes, stirring frequently. Whisk in heavy cream and cook until mixture begins to simmer, 2 to 3 minutes. Remove from heat and stir in ½ cup cheese. Add salt and pepper.

For each Hot Brown, place a slice of toast in an oven-safe dish. Cover with turkey. Place tomato halves alongside. Pour sauce over top to completely cover. Sprinkle with remaining cheese. Place dish under a broiler and cook until cheese begins to bubble and brown. Remove from the broiler, cross two pieces of bacon on top, and sprinkle with paprika and parsley. Serve immediately.

Week Four
TCU vs. Oklahoma State
Stillwater, Oklahoma

Cheese Fries
1 22 oz package frozen waffle fries

Sauce
8 oz Land O Lakes Deli American cubed
½ cup milk
2 tsp dry ranch dressing mix

Topping
6 slices (½ cup) cooked bacon, chopped
¼ cup sliced green onions

Bake waffle fries according to package directions. Meanwhile, whisk milk and ranch dressing together in bowl. Let stand 10 minutes, whisking occasionally. Add cheese. Microwave 1 minute, stir. Continue microwaving 2-3 minutes, stirring every 30 seconds, until melted and smooth. Place hot fries onto serving platter. Top with half of bacon and half of green onions. Drizzle with cheese sauce. Top with remaining bacon and onions. Serve immediately.

Week Five
Clemson vs. Virginia Tech
Blacksburg, Tennessee

622NORTH: Eggs Benedict

1. Tomato Jam

1 ½ cup sun dried tomatoes
4 cloves rough chopped garlic
2 shallots rough chopped
2 ripe tomatoes
½ cup brown sugar
1 cup apple cider vinegar
Salt and pepper

Add all ingredients into a medium sized sauce pan. Simmer on low for 20-30 minutes. Add everything into a food processor or blender; puree. Makes 1 quart. Serves best when warm.

Pesto Hollandaise

6 large egg yolks
1 lemon
½ lb butter (unsalted)
2 oz Basil leaves
1 tsp cayenne
1 tsp salt
1 tsp pepper

In a small saucepan, melt butter over low heat, but do not allow it to brown. Meanwhile, combine other ingredients in food processor/blender. Blend combined ingredients while slowly adding butter over the course of 7 to 8 seconds. Serve immediately. Makes ½ quart.

To poach eggs, bring water and vinegar in a sauce pot to a simmer. Slowly drop egg into water and vinegar, cook until whites are cooked through and the yolk is still runny.

Toast sourdough bread and grill 2 slices of Capicola Ham. Cut sourdough in half and top with Capicola and Tomato Jam. Make a small nest in the tomato jam and gently place poached egg into the jam. Finish with pesto hollandaise.

Week Six
West Virginia vs. TCU
Fort Worth, Texas

El Primos Restaurant:Blue Margarita

1 oz tequila
½ oz roses lime
1½ oz blue margarita mix
½ oz blue curacao
½ oz oj/lime juice mix

Salmon Cancun
6-7 oz salmon
3-4 oz vegetables
3-4 oz Mexican rice
2-3 oz cancun sauce

Cancun Sauce
6 qts heavy cream
½ cup shrimp base
6 cups white wine
1 tbsp white pepper
½ cup rue
(This recipe can be cut in half for a smaller amount).
Rue
Equal parts flour
Equal parts butter

Place marinated salmon on char grill and cook for 10-12 minutes depending on thickness of fillet. Do not overcook. When salmon is 80 percent done start sauce, place diced onions, bell pepper, mushrooms in sauté pan with ½ oz butter, sauté for 2-3 minutes then add shrimp. Continue to sauté until shrimp are cooked, deglaze with 1 oz white wine and add 2 oz Cancun sauce. Remove salmon from grill and place on plate with rice and vegetables and pour sauce over salmon.

Week Seven
Auburn vs. LSU
Baton Rouge, Louisiana

Ruffino's: Cedar Plank Redfish

6 untreated cedar planks (8"to 10" long)
6 (6 oz) fillets of fresh fish
½ cup olive oil
2 tbsp creole seasoning
3 creole seasoning
1 cup basil pesto
½ cup balsamic syrup

Soak the cedar planks in water for at least an hour beforehand. Preheat the grill. Brush the planks with olive oil. Season the fish on both sides with creole seasoning. Lay a fillet in the center of each plank.

Cut the tomatoes in half, lay them on their sides and cut into thin slices. Lay the tomatoes shingle style over the fish, covering the flesh of the fish. Set the planks in the center of the grill and cover immediately. Cook for about 15 minutes or until the fish is cooked and flaky.

There will be a lot of smoke, but this is from the planks smoldering. Serve the planks on a plate and drizzle with pesto and balsamic syrup.

Pastime Lounge: Fried shrimp and oyster Poboy

Vegetable oil, for frying
1 cup all-purpose flour
2 tbsp House Seasoning
3 eggs
1/2 cup hot sauce (recommended: Texas Pete)
7 medium shrimp, peeled

5 medium oysters, shucked
1 hoagie roll, split, buttered and lightly toasted
Tartar Sauce, recipe follows
Shredded lettuce
Sliced tomato
Salt and pepper
Garlic powder

House Seasoning
1 cup salt
1/4 cup black pepper
1/4 cup garlic powder

Heat the oil in a Dutch oven to 375 degrees.Place flour in a bowl and add House Seasoning. In another bowl, beat the eggs and add the hot sauce. Dredge shrimp in egg mixture then the flour mixture and drop into hot oil one at a time. Fry until light brown (do not over cook). Drain on paper towels. Lightly flour oysters and drop one at a time into hot oil. Fry until golden brown and drain. To assemble sandwich, spread both insides of bread with tartar sauce. On the bottom piece, place shredded lettuce and sliced tomato.

Season with salt, pepper and garlic powder to taste. Place oysters on top of tomato. Add another layer of shredded lettuce and then place shrimp on top. Top that with bread and a toothpick to hold the sandwich together.

Week Eight
Michigan vs. Penn State
State College, Pennsylvania

Gabriella's Italian Restaurant:
Penne Vodka Pink Sauce

1 lb penne pasta, cooked aldente
2 tbsp extra virgin olive oil
1 onion, finely chopped
4 garlic cloves, crushed and chopped
2 (28 oz) cans crushed tomatoes
1 pinch hot pepper flakes
3/4 cup vodka (top shelf)
Salt and pepper
2 tbsp fresh parsley, chopped
3/4 cup heavy cream
Parmigiano-reggiano cheese

Put the olive oil into the pan and add the onions and garlic. Turn heat to medium-low and gently cook for a few minutes. Add the red pepper flakes and cook one minute. Add crushed tomatoes. Raise heat to medium and bring the mixture to a boil. Add the vodka and a pinch of salt and pepper simmer uncovered for about eight minutes over medium-low heat.

Add the cream and lower the heat, add drained pasta and toss in parsley. Stir to coat well and grate a generous amount of parmesan into the pasta using micro-plane grater.

Serve immediately sprinkled with more parmesan, and red pepper flakes.

Prime Rib Au Jus
1 (4 to 5-pound) beef rib roast
5 cloves garlic, slivered

1/4 cup peppercorn and garlic marinade (recommended:
McCormick's)
2 tbsp spicy brown mustard
Salt and freshly ground black pepper
2 teaspoons Worcestershire sauce
1/2 cup red wine
1 cup beef broth

Preheat the oven to 350 degrees.

Using a paring knife make small slits into roast about 3-inches
apart and press the garlic slivers into the slits. Using a pastry
brush, coat the entire roast with the mustard. Sprinkle on the
peppercorn and garlic marinade to completely cover the roast.
Place on a rack in a roasting pan and cook until the
thermometer inserted into the center reads 130 degrees.
Remove the roast from the oven, cover with foil and allow to
rest for 10 to 15 minutes.

To make the Au Jus: Place the roasting pan over stovetop
burners on medium low. Whisk in the Worcestershire sauce and
wine and scrape up the little brown bits from the bottom of the
roasting pan. Reduce slightly and add the broth. Bring to a
simmer and reduce slightly. Serve along with the sliced prime
rib.

Week Nine
North Carolina State vs. Notre Dame
South Bend, Indiana

Tippecanoe Place Restaurant:
Lobster cakes

Add butter and oil to a heavy bottom sauce pot and melt over medium heat.
Add garlic and shallot and sweat until shallot are translucent.
Deglaze with champagne and reduce by half.
Add cream, mustard seeds, whole grain mustard and mix well.
Bring to a simmer and cook five minutes.
Add beurre maine to thicken and whisk well to prevent lumps.
Simmer five more minutes until desired consistency is achieved. It should coat the back of the
spoon and when you run your finger across the line, the line should remain and no sauce should run into the line.
Cool down in an ice water bath. Place in an appropriate container, label, wrap and refrigerate overnight.
Reheat and serve as a garnish with the Lobster Cakes.

OPTIONAL: Garnish two Lobster Cakes with the champagne mustard cream sauce on the bed of the plate. Top the cakes with a snap peak, green and yellow pepper salad in a vinaigrette.

Week Ten
LSU vs. Alabama
Tuscaloosa, Alabama

Dreamland: *BBQ Ribs*

Rack of spare ribs
½ cup melted butter or bacon grease
Salt and pepper
Dreamland BBQ sauce

Although the internet recipes use Cattlemen's BBQ or other sauces, it ain't Dreamland unless you use Dreamland sauce. Order at dreamlandbbq.com.

Heat Grill up to High. Remove the membrane off the inside of the rib. Take a filet knife and work between the bone and the membrane until you can get you finger under the membrane. You should be able to easily pull it off once you get hold of it. This is an important step. Brush the ribs with butter or bacon grease and liberally salt, then put on hot grill. Sear both sides of the ribs. You're looking to brown the outsides, not burn them.

Week Eleven
Georgia vs. Auburn
Auburn, Alabama

Momma Goldberg's*: Nachos*

A simple delicacy!
Prep: Only your expectations. This recipe is only a close
second to the real thing.

Original Nacho Cheese Dorito's
Sliced pepper jack cheese
Sliced jalapenos

On a plate, empty one bag of Dorito's. Layer sliced pepper jack
cheese on top of Dorito's until covered to liking. Sliced
jalapenos on top. Place in microwave, watch carefully until
cheese is fully melted. Enjoy.

Week Twelve
Michigan vs. Wisconsin
Madison, Wisconsin

Wisconsin Cheese Curds

Beer battered deep fried cheese curds are a classic Wisconsin appetizer featuring gooey melted cheese waiting to ooze out of a crisp beer-flavored crust!

1 pound cheese curds or cubed mild cheddar
1 cup flour
1 cup beer, plus 1 or 2 tbsp more as needed
1 egg beaten
1 tsp baking powder
1 tsp table salt

Heat oil to 400 degrees.
Mix flour, baking powder and salt together.
Add beaten egg and beer and mix till combined. The batter should have the consistency of thin pancake batter. If it's too thin, add additional beer as needed. If it is still too thin, sprinkle in a little flour.
Deep fry one cheese curd to test the batter if needed.
Working batches, add cheese curds to the batter and evenly coat then lift cheese out of the batter with a spider or slotted spoon and let the excess batter drip off before placing in the oil.
Fry for 1 minute, then remove curds to drain on paper towels.
Let cool slightly and serve.

Note: I found anywhere between 375-400 degrees to be a good frying temperature. Oil temperature drops when food is added, so by heating your oil to 400 degrees it should stay within the proper range when frying. Frying in batches ensures the oil temperature doesn't drop excessively and also ensures the cheese curds aren't too crowded in the pan and clump together. I found one minute to be the ideal cooking time. However, if you see cheese leaking out while frying, they have been frying longer than needed and should be removed.

Week Thirteen
Alabama vs. Auburn
The Iron Bowl
Auburn, Alabama

Acre Restaurant: *Fried Green Tomatoes*

Peanut oil, for frying
12 slices fresh green tomato
1 cup whole buttermilk
2 cups cornmeal, such as Granary Farms
Crystal Rémoulade (recipe follows)
1 cup pimiento cheese
Marinated Crab (recipe follows)
Garnish: fresh basil leaves

In a medium Dutch oven, fill with peanut oil to halfway full.
Heat over medium-high heat until a deep-fry thermometer
reads 350°.

Dip tomato slices in buttermilk; dredge in cornmeal. Cook in
batches until golden brown, approximately two minutes. Let
drain on paper towels.

For each serving, spread 2 tablespoons Crystal Rémoulade on
the bottom of one plate. Top with one tomato slice. Spread
tomato with 2 tbsp pimento cheese. Top with another tomato
slice and 2 tbsp pimiento cheese; top with another tomato slice.
Place ¼ cup Marinated Crab on top of tomato. Garnish with
basil, if desired.

Note: Prepare Crystal Rémoulade and Marinated Crab first.
Pick up store-bought pimiento cheese to save time, or prepare
your family's favorite recipe.

Week Fourteen
SEC Championship
Georgia vs. Auburn
Atlanta, Georgia

Legal Seafood: *Lump Crab Dip*

4 oz cream cheese, softened
1 tbsp heavy cream
1 tbsp grated onion
1 tbsp prepared horseradish
1/2 tsp Old Bay Seasoning
2 oz shredded white cheddar cheese
1 tbsp finely sliced chives
1/2 lb. lump crabmeat

Preheat oven to 350°F.
Combine cream cheese and cream, stirring until smooth.
Stir in onion, horseradish, Old Bay, Cheddar and chives.
Add crabmeat with liquid and fold in gently.
Place in a small baking dish, bake 8-10 minutes or until hot.

Week Fifteen
Army vs. Navy
Philadelphia, Pennsylvania

Osteria: ***World's Best Robiola with Chanterelle Butter Sauce***

Fresh Pasta Dough
6.5 oz flour
2.5 oz durum flour
9 egg yolks
1 tsp extra virgin olive oil
2 tsp cold water

Mix the flours together with the paddle attachment of the Hobart mixer.
Add the yolks, water and olive oil and mix on medium speed until the mixture just begins to combine.
Knead the dough for 4-6 minutes until the gluten begins to properly form and the dough is in one solid piece.
Wrap dough and allow to rest in the refrigerator for at least 30 minutes.

Robiola Filling
3 1 oz squares of Robiola cheese
1 oz Parmesan cheese
1 whole egg
Salt and pepper to taste

Combine above ingredients in a mixing bowl and whisk until smooth and place in a pipping bag.
Roll out pasta dough to desired thickness (thinnest setting), fold in half and mark off edges.
Lightly mist the dough with water and pipe out a small amount of the filling, six in each column.
Fold dough over, and seal each ravioli by pressing out all air, and cut with a fluted edge cutter into the size of postage

stamps.

Chanterelle Butter Sauce
1 oz shaved trumpet mushrooms (cleaned)
3 oz unsalted butter
1 oz extra virgin olive oil
1 clove garlic (crushed)
4-5 thyme sprigs (leaves removed)
2 oz pasta water
Parmesan cheese (as needed)
Salt and pepper to taste

Drop pasta and cook until done (only takes 2 minutes)
In a saute pan, heat olive oil and butter with the crushed garlic;
once the oil is hot, add the thinly shaved trumpets and saute
over medium heat, seasoning with salt, pepper and thyme.
Add pasta water and butter and reduce till a sauce consistency.
Toss the ravioli in the sauce and plate.
Top with parmigiano cheese.

Cheese Steak Sandwich

2 to 2 1/2 pound strip loin, trimmed
Olive oil
Salt and freshly ground black pepper
Soft hoagie rolls, split 3/4 open
Provolone Sauce, recipe follows
Sauteed Mushrooms, recipe follows
Caramelized Onions, recipe follows
Sauteed Peppers, recipe follows

Provolone Sauce
1 tbsp unsalted butter
1 tbsp all-purpose flour
2 cups whole milk, heated

1 cup grated aged provolone cheese
1/4 cup grated Parmigiano-Reggiano
1 tsp kosher salt
1/4 tsp freshly ground black pepper
Sauteed Mushrooms:
2 tablespoons olive oil
1 tablespoon unsalted butter
1 1/2 pounds mushrooms (cremini and shiitake), coarsely
chopped
3 tbsp finely chopped fresh parsley leaves
Salt and freshly ground black pepper

Caramelized Onions
2 tbsp unsalted butter
1 tbsp canola oil
3 large Spanish onions, peeled, halved and thinly sliced
1 tsp kosher salt
1/4 tsp freshly ground black pepper

Sauteed Peppers
2 tbsp olive oil
2 poblano peppers, thinly sliced
2 cubano peppers, thinly sliced
Salt and freshly ground black pepper

Place steak in freezer for 30 to 45 minutes; this makes it easier
to slice the meat. Remove the meat from the freezer and slice
very thinly.

Heat griddle or grill pan over high heat. Brush steak slices with
oil and season with salt and pepper. Cook for 45 to 60 seconds
per side.

Place several slices of the meat on the bottom half of the roll,
spoon some of the cheese sauce over the meat, and top with the
mushrooms, onions, and peppers.

Provolone Sauce
Melt butter in a medium saucepan over medium heat. Whisk in the flour and cook for 1 minute. Slowly whisk in the warm milk, and cook, whisking constantly until thickened, about 4 to 5 minutes. Remove the mixture from the heat and whisk in the provolone and Parmesan until combined; season with salt and pepper.

Sauteed Mushrooms
Heat oil and butter in a large saute pan over high heat. Add the mushrooms and cook until the mushrooms are golden brown. Stir in the parsley and season with salt and pepper.

Caramelized Onions
Heat butter and oil in a large saute pan over medium heat. Add the onions, season with salt and pepper, and cook slowly until golden brown and caramelized, stirring occasionally, approximately 30 to 40 minutes.

Sauteed Peppers
Heat the oil in medium saute pan over high heat. Add the peppers and cook until soft. Season with salt and pepper.

Week Sixteen
Rose Bowl
Georgia vs. Oklahoma
Pasadena, California

Spago: *Wolfgang Puck's Pizzas With Smoked Salmon and Caviar*

1 tbsp minced chives
Pizza dough
4 tbsp extra virgin olive oil
6 tbsp sour cream or creme fraiche
3-4 oz smoked salmon, cut into paper thin slices
4 heaping tbsp domestic golden caviar
1 tsp black caviar

Preheat oven to 500 degrees and put a pizza stone inside.
Knead 2 tablespoons of the minced chives into the pizza dough.
Roll or stretch the dough into four 8in. Circles.
Place the pizzas on a lightly floured wooden peel or board. (Work in batched)
Brush the centers of the circles with olive oil to within 1 inch of the edges.

Slide the pizzas onto the stone and bake 8 to 10 minutes, or until golden brown.
Transfer to serving plates and spread with the sour cream or creme franche.
Arrange the salmon slices over the top.
Place a tablespoon of the golden caviar in the center of each pizza and spoon 1/4 of the black
caviar into each center.
Sprinkle the salmon with the remaining chives and serve!

Pie and Burger: *Fresh Ollallieberry Pie (can substitute blackberries)*

Bake or buy a 10-inch pie shell crust.

Glaze recipe
1 ½ cups of water
1 cup of sugar
2 tsp of red food color
4-5 berries crushed into mixture and stir as you bring to a boil.

Mix 3 oz of corn starch in water making sure to remove all lumps and the mixture is smooth. Slowly add the corn starch to the boiling water while constantly stirring. You want a consistency like a heavy syrup. Take the pie shell and coat the bottom of the shell with the glaze.

You will need three small baskets of berries. And ½ the berries to the shell and cover with the glaze. Add the remaining berries and arrange so the berries are higher in the middle of the shell. Cover completely with the glaze. Make sure not to ignore filling around the outer edge even though there is not as much fruit there. Refrigerate for at least one hour. Serve with fresh ice cream or whipped cream.

Week Seventeen
The National Championship
Georgia vs. Alabama
Atlanta, Georgia

Chops Lobster Bar: *Lobster Mac'n Cheese*

1 quart heavy cream
1 quart half-and-half
1 cup half-and-half
36 oz white cheddar cheese, shredded
4 oz cornstarch
2 tsp kosher salt
1 lb. cavatappi pasta or 1 lb rigatoni pasta
4 oz lobster meat, cooked and cut into small pieces

Mix cornstarch with 2 cups half-and-half in small mixing bowl until smooth. Set aside. Heat remaining half and half with the heavy cream in a large sauce pot to 180 degrees. Add cheese and salt into cream, and whisk until smooth. Add cornstarch and half and half mixture. Stir for 15 minutes over low heat. Add cooked pasta and lobster meat and toss everything in the sauce. Serve.

And that my friends, is the greatest fall of all.